VORTEX

VORTEX

Pound, Eliot, and Lewis

TIMOTHY MATERER

Cornell University Press

ITHACA AND LONDON

First published 1979 by Cornell University Press.
Published in the United Kingdom by Cornell University Press Ltd.,
2-4 Brook Street, London W1Y 1AA.

International Standard Book Number 0-8014-1225-0
Library of Congress Catalog Card Number 79-13009
Printed in the United States of America
*Librarians: Library of Congress cataloging information
appears on the last page of the book.*

Previously unpublished material by Ezra Pound, copyright © 1979 by the Trustees of the Ezra Pound Literary Property Trust. Published by permission of New Directions and Faber & Faber Ltd.

Excerpts from the following works of Ezra Pound are reprinted by permission of New Directions Publishing Corporation: *Pound/Joyce: Letters and Essays,* ed. Forrest Read, copyright © 1965, 1966, 1967, by Ezra Pound; *Gaudier-Brzeska: A Memoir,* copyright © 1970 by Ezra Pound, all rights reserved; *Pavannes and Divagations,* copyright © 1958 by Ezra Pound; *Confucius to Cummings,* ed. Ezra Pound and Marcella Spann, copyright © 1964 by New Directions Publishing Corporation; *The Letters of Wyndham Lewis,* ed. W. K. Rose, copyright © 1963 by Mrs. Wyndham Lewis.

Excerpts from the following works of Ezra Pound are reprinted by permission of New Directions and Faber & Faber Ltd.: *The Cantos,* copyright 1934, 1940, 1948, 1956, © 1962, 1968 by Ezra Pound; *Personae: Collected Shorter Poems,* copyright 1926 by Ezra Pound; *A Lume Spento and Other Early Poems,* copyright © 1965 by Ezra Pound, all rights reserved; *Selected Letters of Ezra Pound, 1907–1941,* ed. D. D. Paige, copyright 1950 by Ezra Pound; *Selected Prose, 1909–1965,* ed. William Cookson, copyright © 1973 by the Trustees of the Ezra Pound Literary Property Trust; *Literary Essays of Ezra Pound,* ed. T. S. Eliot, copyright 1918, 1920, 1935 by Ezra Pound.

Excerpts from *Pound/Joyce: The Letters of Ezra Pound to James Joyce,* ed. Forrest Read, copyright © 1965, 1966, 1967 by Ezra Pound, are reprinted by permission of Faber & Faber Ltd.

Excerpts from Ezra Pound, *The Spirit of Romance,* copyright © 1968 by Ezra Pound, are reprinted by permission of New Directions and Peter Owen Ltd. All rights reserved.

H. D., "Oread," in *Collected Poems,* copyright © 1925, 1953 by Norman Holmes Pearson, is quoted by permission of New Directions.

Excerpts from James Joyce, *Finnegans Wake,* copyright 1939 by James Joyce, © 1967 by George Joyce and Lucia Joyce, are reprinted by permission of the Society of Authors and Viking Press.

TO
MY WIFE,
BARBARA

Contents

Illustrations

Preface

> every thing has its
> Own Vortex; and when once a traveller thro' Eternity
> Has passed that Vortex, he perceives it roll backward behind
> His path, into a globe itself infolding. . . .
> —William Blake, *Milton*

This book examines the artistic crosscurrents in the careers of Ezra Pound, T. S. Eliot, and Wyndham Lewis. Ezra Pound perceived these currents as a vortex, a sign of creative energy, convergence, and order. The work of the sculptor Henri Gaudier-Brzeska was essential to the early days of the Vortex, when Lewis (as both painter and writer) founded the journal *Blast* and the movement called Vorticism in order to revolutionize the arts in England. Gaudier lost his life in World War I, and the movement itself did not survive the cultural disruptions caused by the war. The later history of the Vortex concerns the attempts of Pound, Eliot, and Lewis to rekindle its pre-war energy. Because Pound considered James Joyce a fourth major creator of modern literature, Joyce was potentially a force within the Vortex. The principles that eventually took Joyce out of Pound's orbit help to define through contrast those that held the Vortex together. These aesthetic, social, and philosophical principles run through decades of collaboration and controversy to form the pattern Pound called the Vortex.

Many studies of modern literature have helped me to write this book. I should like to acknowledge particularly Hugh

Kenner's *The Pound Era* and Donald Gallup's *T. S. Eliot and Ezra Pound, Collaborators in Letters.* I am grateful to Donald Eddy and the staff of the Department of Rare Books, Olin Library, Cornell University, and to Peter Dzwonkoski of the Beinecke Library, Yale University, for assistance in using the Pound, Eliot, and Lewis papers in their libraries' collections. For access to the Henri Gaudier material at Kettle's Yard, University of Cambridge, I thank H. S. Ede and Jeremy Lewison, as well as the Kettle's Yard Committee. Summer grants from the National Endowment for the Humanities and the University of Missouri–Columbia Research Council made my work at Kettle's Yard possible. The collections of the Tate Gallery and the Victoria and Albert Museum in London and the John Quinn Archive in the Berg Collection of the New York Public Library were essential to this work. The Research Council of the University of Missouri–Columbia has supported this book at every stage of its composition. I thank Helga Meyer for typing the manuscript.

Excerpts from the works of T. S. Eliot are reprinted by permission of Harcourt Brace Jovanovich, Inc., and Faber & Faber Ltd. Valerie Eliot has kindly allowed me to quote two passages from a letter of 1921 from T. S. Eliot to Wyndham Lewis. Excerpts from the works of Wyndham Lewis are reprinted by permission of the Society of Authors as agents for Gladys Wyndham Lewis. I thank Maurice Beebe for permission to use in revised form materials that originally appeared in the *Journal of Modern Literature* for July 1974 and April 1977.

TIMOTHY MATERER

Columbia, Missouri

VORTEX

1

The Vortex

The form of the arms—a logarithmic spiral—has not as yet given any clue to the dynamics of spiral nebulae. But though we do not understand the cause, we see that there is a widespread law compelling matter to flow in these forms.
—A. S. Eddington, *Stellar Movements and the Structure of the Universe* (1914)

The image of the vortex grew like a crystal in Ezra Pound's mind for over fifty years. He writes in his 1908 poem "Plotinus":

As one that would draw through the node of things,
Back-sweeping to the vortex of the cone
. . .
I was an atom on creation's throne. . . .[1]

The poem draws on Plotinus's description of the soul's inherently circular motion "about the source of its own existence." The word *vortex,* however, comes not from Plotinus but from the pre-Socratic doctrine that the four elements were formed as they rotated in a vortex or *dine.*[2] From Allen Upward's *New Word* (1908), Pound learned that

1. Ezra Pound, *A Lume Spento and Other Early Poems* (New York: New Directions, 1965), p. 56. Pound learned of the origin of the term from John Burnet's *Early Greek Philosophy* (1892). Pound wrote in 1916 that his "first connection with vorticist movement" came when he was less than two years old, "during the Great Blizzard of '87 when I came East . . . behind the first rotary snow-plough" (C. David Heyman, *Ezra Pound: The Last Rower, A Political Profile* [New York: Viking Press, 1976], p. 4).
2. See my "Pound's Vortex," *Paideuma* 6 (Fall 1977):175–76.

the double vortex of a waterspout expresses "the true beat of strength, the first beat . . . which we feel in all things that come within our measure, in ourselves, and in our starry world."[3] Upward claimed the "fair probability" that organic life on earth sprang from "minute cosmic individuals, endowed with energy of their own, similar in origin and character to that manifested in the rotary or vortical motion of the planets." He called these strange energy units "vorticells" and would no doubt have considered that the discovery of the helical structure of the DNA model supported his theory.[4] His reference to the "vortical movement" in "our starry world" is to the spiral patterns that nineteenth-century astronomers, as if expanding pre-Socratic theories, began to discover in many star systems. The presence of a "vortex" in both DNA and the Andromeda galaxy indicates the kind of "patterned energy" that Pound could trace through such disparate objects as a plate of metal filings and a rose—a rose, that is, such as a Vorticist artist might draw (Fig. 1).

"Plotinus" shows that Pound used the vortex image well before 1914, when he applied it to a group of painters led by Wyndham Lewis, the Vorticists. Lewis himself was using a vortex motif in his drawings as early as 1912. He was influenced by the London exhibitions of Italian Futurists in 1912 and 1913, especially by Umberto Boccioni's *States of Mind* series, and he may have known Giacomo Balla's *Vortice* paintings.[5] Lewis used a vortex design brilliantly in

3. Allen Upward, *The New Word* (London: A. C. Fifield, 1908), p. 195.
4. Allen Upward, "The Nebular Origin of Life," *New Age* 30 (January 5, 1922):116. Concerning Upward and DNA, see Donald Davie, *Ezra Pound* (New York: Viking Press, 1975), p. 67.
5. Richard Cork, *Vorticism and Abstract Art in the First Machine Age,* 2 vols. (Berkeley and Los Angeles: University of California Press, 1976), vol. 1, pp. 255–56. According to Charles Marriott in *Modern Movements in Painting* (London: Chapman & Hall, 1920, p. 160), the Futurist artist C. D. Carrà used the word *vortex* to describe "the emotional condition of

1. Abstract design from *Blast*, no. 1.
Olin Library, Cornell University.

his *Timon of Athens* illustrations, which were highly praised when exhibited at Roger Fry's Second Post-Impressionist show in 1912. In one of these designs for Shakespeare's play, the geometrical shapes of armored figures are engulfed in a whirlwind that draws them to the center of the vortex. In a nearly abstract design, which Pound considered the best in the *Timon* series, the human forms seem like fragments from an explosion (Fig. 2). Pound said that the work's theme was the "fury of intelligence baffled and shut in by circumjacent stupidity."[6] Lewis's vortex is a satiric whirlwind directed at such stupidity, as if Timon's enemies were the subject of T. S. Eliot's lines:

> Whirled in a vortex which shall bring
> The world to that destructive fire . . .[7]

Yet Lewis's vortex was also creative. Along with the *Timon* drawings, Lewis exhibited in 1912 a painting called *Creation,* which shows a highly stylized male and female couple engaged in a fertility dance within its whirling planes. Lewis returned to this combination of the creation theme and vortex design throughout his career. In *Creation Myth No. 17* (1941), a stream of organic matter shoots off into space from a turning, tightly packed nucleus of semiabstract but clearly living forms. In *What the Sea Is Like at Night* (1949), the vast power of the swirling ocean is nevertheless unable to obliterate the animal-like forms that ride the

the Futurist" in his contribution to Boccioni's *Pittura, Scultura Futuriste (Dinamismo Plastico)* in 1914.

6. Ezra Pound, *Gaudier-Brzeska: A Memoir* (New York: New Directions, 1970), p. 93.

7. T. S. Eliot, "East Coker," *Collected Poems, 1909–1962* (New York: Harcourt Brace Jovanovich, 1963), p. 184.

2. Wyndham Lewis, *Composition: Timon of Athens.* Herbert F. Johnson
Museum of Art, Cornell University. Photo by Jon Reis.

currents.[8] Lewis's novels as well as his paintings stress the necessary violence and destructiveness that accompany any creative act. The energy needed for either creation or destruction fascinated him.

Pound thought that "the thing that matters in art is a sort of energy."[9] He briefly defined the vortex as "the point of maximum energy" and, in a fuller definition, related it to the image: "The image is not an idea. It is a radiant node or cluster; it is a . . . VORTEX, from which, and through which, and into which, ideas are constantly rushing."[10] The reference to "node" recalls the "Plotinus" poem and suggests, as do the echoes of the Minor Elevation of the Mass, that the vortex continues to have mystical significance for Pound. His alliance with Vorticism, however, had the immediate, practical purpose of extricating him from the Imagist movement, which had been taken over by the "hippopoetess" Amy Lowell. He cut his ties with Lowell as Lewis used Vorticism to cut his with Roger Fry and the Omega Workshops. To effect this break, Pound did not need to change his Imagist tenets; he merely changed the movement's name. He wrote to Harriet Monroe that an article on "Imagisme" would appear under the altered title of "Vorticism."[11] Pound used the term *vortex* quite subjectively to describe the creative energy he thought the Imagists lacked, as in this description of Lewis's art in a letter to John Quinn: "It is not merely knowledge of technique, or skill, it is intelligence and

8. Lewis's paintings are reproduced in Walter Michel, *Wyndham Lewis: Paintings and Drawings* (Berkeley and Los Angeles: University of California Press, 1971).

9. Pound, *Literary Essays of Ezra Pound,* ed. T. S. Eliot (New York: New Directions, 1968), p. 49.

10. Pound, *Gaudier-Brzeska,* pp. 81, 92.

11. Pound to Monroe, 1914, Harriet Monroe Collection, University of Chicago Library.

knowledge of life, of the whole of it, beauty, heaven, hell, sarcasm, every kind of whirlwind of force and emotion. Vortex. That is the right word, if I did find it myself."[12]

Pound met Lewis in 1909 through Laurence Binyon at the Vienna Café, where British Museum curators such as Binyon and voracious readers such as Lewis would gather. Pound recalls in Canto 80:

> So it is to Mr. Binyon that I owe, initially,
> Mr. Lewis. . . . His bull-dog me,
> as it were against old Sturge M's bull-dog. . . .

The spirit of rivalry that arose from the artists' identification as the protégés (or "prodigies," to use Pound's word) of the poet and the scholar (Lewis as T. Sturge Moore's "bull-dog," Pound as Binyon's) did as little to foster their association as Pound's dubious sense of humor. Lewis recalled that on one of their first meetings at the café Pound remarked:

> "This young man could probably tell you!" . . . with a great archness, narrowing his eyes and regarding me with mischievous goodwill.
>
> There had been some question of the whereabouts of a kidnapped or absconding prostitute. Ezra was already attributing to those he liked proclivities which he was persuaded must accompany the revolutionary intellect.[13]

Lewis often felt uncomfortable with the poet he called the "Trotsky of Literature." But as friends of Ford Madox Ford and contributors to Ford's *English Review,* they met at South Lodge as well as the Vienna Café; and Pound was

12. Pound, *Selected Letters of Ezra Pound, 1907–1941,* ed. D. D. Paige (New York: New Directions, 1971), p. 74.
13. Lewis, *Blasting and Bombardiering* (London: Eyre & Spottiswoode, 1937), p. 277.

introduced to Lewis's "sculptural" qualities as a painter by Jacob Epstein.[14] Their friendship grew closer in 1914 during the days of Vorticism and its journal, *Blast*.

In March 1914 Lewis founded the Rebel Art Centre, which he hoped would rival Roger Fry's "curtain and pincushion factory," the Omega Workshops. The original rebels were a group of painters who noisily resigned from the Omega with Lewis—Frederick Etchells, Cuthbert Hamilton, Charles Nevinson (soon to become a Futurist), and Edward Wadsworth. Besides being a rallying point for the painters, the Rebel Art Centre announced that it would, "by public discussion, lectures and gatherings of people, familiarize those who are interested with the ideas of the great modern revolution."[15] Pound first joined the rebels as a lecturer on the "revolution" and delivered what was to be his "Vorticism" essay. The name Vorticism was not applied to the rebel movement until most of *Blast* was already printed. To the sheets printed, new ones were added that defined the rebels' outlook as "Vorticist."[16] The last-minute use of the term may suggest some doubt, perhaps on Lewis's part, of its usefulness. Lewis may have been wary of Pound's taste for propaganda, as he was reportedly upset when Pound hung a banner proclaiming "END OF CHRISTIAN ERA" at the Rebel Art Centre.[17] Lewis nevertheless recognized the need for a name more specific than "rebel." In one of the *Blast* pages that were printed before the new name was adopted, Lewis wrote that a term better than "Futurist" should be found to identify the painter who is "occupying himself with questions of a renova-

14. See Pound, *Selected Letters,* p. 74.
15. Quoted in Michel, *Wyndham Lewis,* pp. 70–71.
16. Ibid.
17. See W. K. Rose, "Ezra Pound and Wyndham Lewis: The Crucial Years," *Southern Review* 4 (Winter 1968):84.

tion of art, and showing a tendency to rebellion against the domination of the Past."[18]

Soon Vorticism was no longer interchangeable with Imagism or so readily confused with Futurism. When Pound redefines the image as a vortex in his "Vorticism" essay, he quotes Thomas Aquinas to the effect that names depend on the things they denote. The name Vorticism is superior to Imagism because it suggests the greater energy of the poetic image as the Vorticist uses it (that is, as Ezra Pound uses it). Pound seems to redefine Imagism in terms of *energeia,* which Aristotle defined (*Rhetoric* III, xi) as making one's hearer "see things" by "using expressions that represent things as in a state of activity." The new term "Vorticism" had the further advantage that it could be applied to all of the arts. This flexibility (or, as Lewis may have felt, vagueness) became important as the movement expanded. The French sculptor Henri Gaudier-Brzeska had come to London in 1910, joined the Omega, and met Pound at an exhibition in 1913. Pound admired Gaudier's primitivistic style, which was similar to Epstein's though more gentle in spirit and sensitive in line, and generously bought and commissioned works from him. Although Lewis thought Gaudier too gentle to be a true Vorticist, the sculptor soon aligned himself with the rebels and *Blast.* In Pound's eyes, the center of the movement consisted of Lewis (a painter), Gaudier-Brzeska (a sculptor), and himself. Such prose writers as Ford Madox Ford and Rebecca West were accommodated in *Blast,* however, and the Rebel Art Centre's prospectus even promised lectures by "some great innovator in music, Schoenburg or Scrabine [sic]."[19]

18. Lewis, *Wyndham Lewis on Art,* ed. Walter Michel and C. J. Fox (New York: Funk & Wagnalls, 1969), p. 47.
19. Quoted in William C. Wees, *Vorticism and the English Avant-Garde* (Manchester: Manchester University Press, 1972), p. 70.

Pound's definition of the Vortex, which he developed in a section of *Blast* called "VORTEX. POUND.," offered avant-garde artists in all art forms the sense of a common goal. Pound, Lewis, and Gaudier each stated his own "Vortex" or artistic credo in *Blast.* Perhaps the rebels noticed that it was only a step from "vortex" to "vor-text," a foreword (*Vorwort*), pre-text, or statement of first principles. Pound's brilliant perception of the unity of the avant-garde movement justifies the rubric "Vortex" for his statement: "Every concept, every emotion presents itself to the vivid consciousness in some primary form. It belongs to the art of this form. If sound, to music; if formed words, to literature; the image, to poetry . . . colour in position, to painting; form or design in three planes, to sculpture. . . ."[20] This statement not only allows the arts to work together but shows that they exist on equal terms. This aesthetic would eliminate the nineteenth-century tendency to paint literary pictures or write pictorial verse. Whatever his art, the Vorticist uses "primary form." Pound's features may be recognizable in Gaudier's *Hieratic Head of Ezra Pound,* but the emphasis falls on the realtion-ship of the curved masses of the hair, the domed forehead and slitted eyes, and the geometrically shaped nose, mouth, and goatee. More radically, Lewis's *Composition in Blue* presents entirely nonrepresentational shapes that exist only to set off the area of blue watercolor against the black lines and shadings of the composition. In what could be a comment on this severe design, Pound wrote that "Vorticism is art before it has spread itself into flaccidity, into elaboration and secondary applications."[21] Such totally abstract canvases showed that Vorticism was original and powerful enough to distinguish itself from Futurism and even Cubism.

20. "VORTEX POUND.," *Blast,* no. 1 (June 20, 1914), p. 154.
21. *Gaudier-Brzeska,* p. 88.

The challenge of this uncompromising use of pure form was one of the motivating forces behind Pound's *Cantos*.[22]

Vorticism not only tried to bridge the gap between the visual and the verbal arts; it also hoped to humanize the quantitative world of the sciences. In the "Vorticism" essay, Pound gives us the mathematical formula for the circle, which represents "the circle free of space and time limits," and declares that "great works of art contain this . . . sort of equation. They cause form to come into being. By the 'image' I mean such an equation."[23] At this point in the essay, he redefines the image as the vortex. The term is ideal because a vortex represents a pattern of energies, as it does in the whirlwind of forces in Lewis's *Timon*; and patterned energies also constitute the physical world. Pound writes that science reveals "a world of moving energies . . . magnetisms that take form."[24] The Vorticists intended to express this world in their art. As one critic of Vorticism writes, "Recent advances and popularizations of physics had forced many, like Henry Adams, to quail before the 'new multiverse of forces,' but the Vorticists had no such fears and gladly took on the task of conceptualizing this new world as a world of forms."[25] Pound found support for his beliefs in Allen Upward, and Lewis, as some of the spiral forms in his paintings suggest, in the discoveries of such astronomers as A. S. Eddington. The title of Lewis's Vorticist play, *Enemy of the Stars,* was inspired by the binary star Algol, which is regularly eclipsed by a dimmer star. The play's protagonist, Arghol, embodies the artist, who is certain to be misunder-

22. See Ronald Bush, *The Genesis of Ezra Pound's Cantos* (Princeton, N.J: Princeton University Press, 1976), chap. 2.
23. *Gaudier-Brzeska*, pp. 91–92.
24. Pound, *Literary Essays*, p. 154.
25. Herbert N. Schneidau, "Vorticism and the Career of Ezra Pound," *Modern Philology* 65 (February 1968):221.

stood and eventually blacked out. The play does not concern realistic or even human characters; it dramatizes the conflict of the abstract forces of creation and destruction.

If the Vorticists did not fear the "multiverse of forces," neither did they fear the world that machines and industrialism were creating. "'Vorticism,'" Lewis wrote in a 1939 reminiscence, "accepted the machine world; that is the point to stress."[26] Lewis was opposing Herbert Read's claim that the abstract artist was fleeing from the mechanized world of science into an imaginary world. The Vorticist Manifesto, on the contrary, asserted that the modern artist is inspired by "the forms of machinery, Factories, new and vaster buildings, bridges and works."[27] The clear lines of force revealed by a machine's levers and gears suggested a new language of form. The Vorticists did not deny that the landscapes created by industrialism were generally hideous. But the Vortex would sweep up this ugliness, blast it to pieces, and assemble it in beautiful painted forms. In *Blast,* no. 1, Lewis writes that "a man could make just as fine an art in discords, and with nothing but 'ugly' trivial and terrible materials, as any classic artist did with only 'beautiful' and pleasant means."[28]

An "art in discords" recalls the finest pieces of verbal art *Blast* offered, T. S. Eliot's "Preludes" and "Rhapsody on a Windy Night." Neither Pound nor Lewis knew Eliot at the time of *Blast,* no. 1 (June 1914). Pound met Eliot in the fall of 1914 and shortly thereafter invited Lewis to his triangular flat in Kensington to meet, as Lewis writes, "the author of *Prufrock*—indeed . . . Prufrock himself: but a Prufrock to whom the mermaids would decidedly have sung."[29] Although Eliot was still studying at Oxford, he followed the

26. *Wyndham Lewis on Art,* p. 340.
27. Ibid., p. 30.
28. Ibid., p. 50.
29. Lewis, *Blasting and Bombardiering,* p. 284.

Vorticists' activities in London and tried to break into *Blast* with appropriately energetic poems. "I have corresponded with Lewis," Eliot wrote to Pound, "but his Puritanical Principles seem to bar my way to Publicity. I fear that King Bolo and his Big Black Kween will never burst into print." [30] Lewis told Pound that he wished to use Eliot's "excellent bits of scholarly ribaldry . . . but stick to my naïf determination to have no 'words ending in -Uck, -Unt, and -Ugger.'" [31]

"Preludes" made a positive contribution to the Vorticist cause such as "King Bolo," one suspects, could not have. Eliot's poems were the only literary productions in *Blast* that matched in force and originality the designs of Lewis, Gaudier-Brzeska, and the painter Edward Wadsworth. *Blast,* no. 1, did print a section of Ford Madox Ford's *The Good Soldier,* which was then entitled *The Saddest Story.* But the novel's prose seems tame next to the Vorticists' "Blasts" and Lewis's *Enemy of the Stars,* and its technical innovations were not apparent in a brief excerpt. Ford's experience with the Vorticists seems to be summed up by the occasion when, while he was lecturing in a frock coat at the Rebel Art Centre, Lewis's abstract canvas *Plan of War* toppled onto Ford's head and momentarily perched there, harmlessly but ridiculously. As for Pound, Lewis was right when he commented years later that Pound's "fire-eating propagandist utterances were not accompanied by any very experimental efforts in his particular medium." [32] Pound mixed awkward satire ("Let us deride the smugness of 'The Times': / GUFFAW!") with uninspired attempts to use primary form (as in the two-line poem "L'Art": "Green arsenic smeared on an

30. "A Bundle of Letters," in Ezra Pound, *Perspectives,* ed. Noel Stock (Chicago: Henry Regnery, 1965), p. 111.
31. Lewis, *The Letters of Wyndham Lewis,* ed. W. K. Rose (New Directions, 1963), pp. 66–67.
32. Wyndham Lewis, *Time and Western Man* (London: Chatto & Windus, 1927), p. 55.

egg-white cloth, / Crushed strawberries! Come, let us feast our eyes."[33]

Unlike Ezra Pound's poems, Eliot's were both compressed and vivid enough to seem, at least, inspired by the Vorticist aesthetic of primary form. In them modern urban life is an assemblage of "sordid images." "Preludes" presents a stylized rather than a realistic character:

> You had such a vision of the street
> As the street hardly understands;
> Sitting along the bed's edge, where
> You curled the papers from your hair,
> Or clasped the yellow soles of feet
> In the palms of both soiled hands.[34]

There is a *fin de siècle* quality about Eliot's subject, as if the woman in these lines came from a painting by Walter Sickert. Nor does the poem contain the aggressive energy Pound and Lewis desired; Eliot's urban world is dispiriting rather than inspiring. T. S. Eliot was never a Vorticist in the sense of a modern who accepts the machine age and the "new multiverse of forces." T. E. Hulme might have been speaking for Eliot in 1915 when he rejected the symbol of the spiral, with its implication of progress and optimism, in favor of the wheel: "this realisation of the *tragic* significance of life . . . has formed the basis of all the great religions, and is most conveniently remembered by the symbol of the *wheel*." He suggests that this symbol is "lost to the modern world, nor can it be recovered without great difficulty."[35] Eliot was to recover it, however, in *Four Quartets*.

33. Pound, "L'Art, 1910," *Personae: Collected Shorter Poems* (New York: New Directions, 1926), p. 113.
34. Eliot, "Preludes," in *Collected Poems,* p. 14.
35. T. E. Hulme, "A Notebook by T. E. H.," *New Age* 18 (December 23, 1915):188.

If Eliot was not temperamentally a Vorticist, he was nevertheless a part of what Pound called "our little gang." When Dorothy Shakespear Pound painted her *Hommages—to Vorticism,* she used the initials of Pound, Lewis, Gaudier-Brzeska, and Eliot in her design.[36] Her painting represents Ezra Pound's sense of the four artists essential to Vorticism as a new movement in the arts. Although Eliot's character never seemed energetic enough to Pound and Lewis, his art unquestionably had the distinct and vivid quality of *energeia.* The verbs "sitting," "curled," and "clasped" and the images of "yellow soles" and "soiled hands" powerfully convey the emptiness of the woman's life in a poem nearly as free of representative or narrative qualities as an abstract canvas. Like the Vorticist painting of Pound's formulation, Eliot's art had not "spread itself into . . . elaboration and secondary application."

Eliot joined the Vorticists as the movement was being engulfed by World War I. In *Blast*'s second issue, following a "Vortex" sent from France by Gaudier-Brzeska, appears the black-bordered notice: "MORT POUR LA PATRIE. Henri Gaudier-Brzeska: after months of fighting and two promotions for gallantry."[37] Soon Lewis had also joined the army. As Lewis wrote in his final editorial, "BLAST finds itself surrounded by a multitude of other Blasts. . . . [It] will, however, try and brave the waves of blood, for the serious mission it has on the other side of World War."[38]

By dispersing the Vortex, World War I destroyed England's hope for a new renaissance; at least this was Pound's

36. Dorothy Shakespear Pound, *Etruscan Gate: A Notebook with Drawings and Watercolors,* ed. Moelwyn Merchant (Exeter: Rougemont Press, 1971).
37. *Blast,* no. 2, p. 34.
38. Ibid., p. 5.

and Lewis's opinion. In February of 1915, Pound could still write: "New masses of unexplored arts and facts are pouring into the vortex of London. They cannot help bringing about changes as great as the Renaissance changes."[39] The Vorticists were in effect following Pound's prescriptions for the making of a renaissance, as he outlined them in *Patria Mia* (1913). First, dead ideas must be demolished: "A *Risorgimento* implies a whole volley of liberations; liberations from ideas, from stupidities."[40] By its very name, *Blast* promised to do this demolishing and at the same time to liberate the energy needed to produce new life. Pound recalled that the title *Blast* was "connected in the arcane recesses of Mr. Lewis's mind with blastoderms and sources of life."[41] *Blast* also provided two more essentials for a renaissance, "enthusiasm and a propaganda."[42]

A major target of the Vorticists was the Victorian age, as in this editorial "BLAST" from Lewis:

BLAST

years 1837 to 1900 . . .

BLAST their weeping whiskers—hirsute

RHETORIC of EUNUCH and STYLIST—

SENTIMENTAL HYGIENICS

ROUSSEAUISMS (wild Nature cranks)

FRATERNIZING WITH MONKEYS . . .[43]

To proclaim this break with the past, Pound hung out his "END OF CHRISTIAN ERA" banner; and even though Lewis

39. *Gaudier-Brzeska,* p. 117.

40. Pound, *Patria Mia,* in *Selected Prose, 1909–1965,* ed. William Cookson (New York: New Directions, 1973), p. 112. Although this work was first published in 1950, it was written in 1913.

41. Ezra Pound, *If This Be Treason* (Siena: printed for Olga Rudge by Tipografia Nuova, 1948), p. 29.

42. Pound, *Selected Prose,* p. 128.

43. *Blast,* no. 1, p. 18.

disliked its sensationalism, he entirely agreed with its message. With the remnants of Victorianism cleared away, the arts could lead the way to a remade culture: "This will have its effect not only in the arts," Pound wrote of his renaissance, "but in life, in politics, and in economics. If I seem to lay undue stress upon the status of the arts, it is only because the arts respond to an intellectual movement more swiftly and more apparently than do institutions."[44] In 1939 Lewis reflected on the intense hopes of the *Blast* days and compared his zeal to that of the early Christians, although a more relevant comparison could be made to Percy Bysshe Shelley or Thomas Carlyle. He writes here in the third person in order to dissociate himself from the naiveté of his earlier character: "He thought the time had come to shatter the visible world to bits, and build it nearer to the heart's desire: and he really was persuaded that this *absolute* transformation was imminent. . . . The War looked to him like an episode at first—rather proving his contentions than otherwise."[45] The Vorticists imagined that the war might finish the job of demolishing the premodern era that they had begun. With terrible irony, Gaudier-Brzeska wrote in the "VORTEX" he sent from France just before his death: "THIS WAR IS A GREAT REMEDY."[46]

When Lewis himself went to the front in 1917, he quickly lost any illusions about the "remedial" nature of the war. He saw heavy combat before he was transferred to Lord Beaverbrook's Canadian War Memorials project. (The critic T. E. Hulme was killed in a battery less than a quarter mile from Lewis's own.) Lewis wrote in 1939 that he understood the war's significance when "he found himself in the mud of

44. Pound, *Selected Prose,* pp. 111–12.
45. *Wyndham Lewis on Art,* p. 340.
46. *Blast,* no. 2, p. 33.

Passchendaele" and realized that "the community to which he belonged would never be the same again: and that all *surplus* vigour was being bled away and stamped out."[47]

Yet Ezra Pound had vigor to spare. His crucial services to Eliot, Joyce, and a dozen other writers (both great and insignificant) are legendary. Lewis describes him in *Blast* as a "demon pantechnicon driver, busy with removal of old world into new quarters," and Pound told Joyce in 1917 that the description was "becoming daily more apt."[48] He arranged sales of both Lewis's and Gaudier's works to John Quinn and proposed using Quinn's money for a third issue of *Blast*. Pound sent Lewis long letters of medical advice, worked to have him transferred out of the artillery, and would have been his biographer and legal executor had Lewis been killed. When Lewis returned safely from the war, Pound was eager to get on with the revolution.

Despite Lewis's bitterness over the "mud of Passchendaele," much of his vigor, or Vorticist energy, did in fact survive the war. His works contained "the thought of the modern and the energy of the cave-man," Eliot wrote in 1918.[49] Although Lewis was full of schemes to rebuild the visual world, the real problem was to activate them. Plans for a new issue of *Blast* fell through. Some of the Vorticist painters, including Lewis and Edward Wadsworth, reassembled as Group X, but they broke up after one exhibition. The conservative turn that Lewis's painting took as he moved away from abstraction undoubtedly deprived the movement of some of its urgency and originality. As Richard Cork has shown, the Vorticist painters were unified by

47. *Wyndham Lewis on Art*, p. 340.
48. *Blast*, no. 1, p. 82; *Pound/Joyce: Letters and Essays*, ed. Forrest Read (New York: New Directions, 1970), p. 112.
49. Eliot, "Tarr," *Egoist* 5 (September 1918):3.

Lewis's leadership rather than by a substantial aesthetic agreement among them. In regard to literary art, Pound, Lewis, and Eliot could at least publish together in *The Little Review,* which Pound announced as "a place where the current prose writings of James Joyce, Wyndham Lewis, T. S. Eliot, and myself might appear regularly, promptly, and together."[50] Yet neither Pound nor Lewis felt that they were making significant progress. The war had left the cultural community economically and culturally depressed. It indeed had no "surplus vigour" for the revolution.

Lewis dreamed of a society that would support a rebirth of culture such as the Vorticists projected. In 1919 he published a short book, *The Caliph's Design: Architects! Where Is Your Vortex?* which presents his "parable" of a strong ruler who imposes the conditions necessary for a renewed culture. Lewis imagines his Caliph rising one morning, sketching out some strange designs, and then summoning his chief engineer and architect. He tells them that his city bores him, "'so I have done a design of a new city, or rather of a typical street in a new city. It is a little vorticist bagatelle.'" The Caliph's men are amused and puzzled, then terrified as they learn that they have only a few hours "'to invent the forms and conditions that would make it possible to realize my design.'" If they fail, their "'heads will fall.'" Under these conditions, the job gets done: "And within a month a strange street transfigured the heart of that cultivated city."[51] Perhaps in the back of Lewis's mind was the memory of the commission from Lord Beaverbrook that had rescued him from the trenches and set him painting rather than firing howitzers. But the interventions of such powerful art patrons are rare. Until one came along, Lewis was content to go

50. Pound, "Editorial," *Little Review* 4 (May 1917):3.
51. *Wyndham Lewis on Art,* pp. 133–34.

"underground," as he put it, and study the techniques of draftsmanship that he felt he had neglected during his Vorticist period.

Pound was not so patient. His place was in the center of artistic life, not "underground." In 1920, as correspondent for the *Dial,* he worked for an international literary culture rather than a national or English-language one. In addition to contributions from Lewis, Eliot, and Joyce, he was acquiring works from Julien Benda, Miguel Unamuno, Paul Valéry, and Louis Aragon.[52] Even by 1916 Pound had probably started on what he called his "farewell to London," *Hugh Selwyn Mauberley.* Hugh Kenner calls *Mauberley* "an elegy for the Vortex."[53] Section V is an elegy for such men as Gaudier-Brzeska, who died before they could remake a moribund culture:

> There died a myriad,
> And of the best, among them,
> For an old bitch gone in the teeth,
> For a botched civilization. . . .

Kenner says that there "was no more Vortex after 1919, and they went each his own way from that common memory."[54] Yet the Vortex did not entirely dissolve in 1919. The "common memory" was a powerful, magnetic force for Pound, Eliot, and Lewis. Kenner further believes that "what cost all of them so much lost effort . . . was the dissipation of the Vortex: the necessity, all the latter part of their lives, of working alone."[55] They would have worked alone in any

52. Noel Stock, *The Life of Ezra Pound* (New York: Random House, 1970), p. 233.
53. Hugh Kenner, *The Pound Era* (Berkeley and Los Angeles: University of California Press, 1971), p. 287.
54. Ibid., p. 553.
55. Ibid., p. 555.

case; their individuality was too great to permit them to work as a unit. From the beginning, Pound announced that "the Vorticist movement is a movement of individuals, for individuals, for the production of individuality."[56] In his journal *The Exile,* Pound wrote, "I don't think I have ever agreed with Mr. Lewis or Mr. Joyce about anything, certainly not about any basic idea or 'relation to life,'" and he continued that he rarely agreed with Mr. Eliot.[57] All one could ask, Pound said, was for men who received experiences in "modalities" different from one's own to report and debate their findings. He scolded a friend for wanting to find a group of men who shared his ideas: "How the hell many points of agreement do you suppose there were between Joyce, W. Lewis, Eliot and yrs. truly in 1917, or between Gaudier and Lewis in 1913 . . . ?" He told his naive correspondent that "if another man has ideas of *any* kind (not borrowed clichés) that irritate you enough to make you think or take out your own ideas and look at 'em, that is all one can expect."[58]

The Vortex was never a "group," in the sense one applies the term to the Bloomsbury or Auden groups. George Orwell observes how easily such writers as W. H. Auden and Stephen Spender, less gifted than the writers of the twenties, fall into a group: "Technically they are closer together, politically they are almost indistinguishable, and their criticisms of one another's work have always been (to put it mildly) good-natured."[59] To put it mildly, the Vortex's criticism of their own works was never even tactful—

56. Pound, "Edward Wadsworth, Vorticist," *Egoist* 1 (August 15, 1914):306.
57. Pound, "Data," *Exile,* no. 4 (Autumn 1928), pp. 106–7.
58. *Selected Letters of Ezra Pound,* p. 222.
59. George Orwell, "Inside the Whale," in *Collected Essays* (London: Secker & Warburg, 1961), p. 140.

Pound's term for it was "eye-gouging," which he considered a good thing. Pound never tired of baiting "Possum" Eliot, who had attained his eminence as a literary critic "largely through disguising himself as a corpse," and Eliot chose Pound as one of his prime "heretics" in *After Strange Gods,* characterizing the author of *The Cantos* as "attracted to the Middle Ages, apparently, by everything except that which gives them their significance."[60] In his self-conceived role as the "Enemy," Lewis attacked Pound as a "revolutionary simpleton" and Eliot as a "pseudoist."

None of this criticism was taken personally—or at least not for long. Pound thought that the flaw in William Carlos Williams's criticism of Eliot was that "it's personal, not opposition."[61] Although Lewis is often characterized as a maliciously personal critic, Eliot and Pound understood that Lewis always put the issue before the personality. In acknowledging Lewis's attacks upon him, Eliot wrote that Lewis was always "impartial" and that "at no time do I remember his wit as having any savour of malice."[62] The meaning of "opposition" is that one chooses worthy opponents—people with ideas and not "borrowed clichés." Both Pound and Eliot, for example, criticized Lewis for wasting his time attacking the Sitwells. In *After Strange Gods,* Eliot explained that he had criticized only great writers: "for my purpose the second-rate were useless."[63]

This distinction between a "vortex" of original and inde-

60. Pound, "Credo," as quoted in Stock, *Life of Ezra Pound,* p. 295; Eliot, *After Strange Gods* (New York: Harcourt Brace, 1934), p. 45. For Pound's reference to "eye-gouging," see Harry M. Meacham, *The Caged Panther: Ezra Pound at St. Elizabeths* (New York: Twayne, 1967), p. 140.
61. *Charles Olson and Ezra Pound: An Encounter at St. Elizabeths,* ed. Catherine Seelye (New York: Viking Press, 1975), p. 86.
62. Eliot, "Wyndham Lewis," *Hudson Review* 10 (Summer 1957):169.
63. Eliot, *After Strange Gods,* p. 9.

pendent minds and a mere "group" is necessary if we are to understand the lifelong relationship of Eliot, Pound, and Lewis. As a continuing clash of energetic minds, the Vortex did not die in 1919. The first short-lived phase of the Vortex and the long, slowly decelerating one that followed correspond to what Pound called the first two phases of "Kulchur": "the nineteen teens, Gaudier, Wyndham L. and I as we were in *Blast,* and the next phase, the 1920's. The sorting out, the *rappel à l'ordre.*"[64]

64. Pound, *Guide to Kulchur* (New York: New Directions, 1968), p. 95. Pound borrows the phrase *rappel à l'ordre* from Jean Cocteau.

2

The Vortex as a
Pattern of Hope

Myth grows spiral-wise . . . it closely corresponds, in the
realm of the spoken word, to a crystal in the realm of physical
matter.
　　　　　　　—Claude Lévi-Strauss, *Structural Anthropology*

While Ezra Pound was contemplating his break with
London, T. S. Eliot and Wyndham Lewis were drawing
closer together. They took a holiday in France together in
the summer of 1920 and delivered a present from Ezra
Pound to James Joyce in Paris (which embarrassingly turned
out to be a used pair of brown shoes).[1] They toured the Loire
valley, where Lewis gave Eliot lessons in landscape sketching; and they were amused with each other's peculiarities,
such as Lewis's exaggerated fear of infection after a bicycle
accident and Eliot's meticulous totting up of each day's
expenses.[2]

In London they searched for financial backing for a
journal. Because a vortex is a confluence of forces, it needs a
center from which to circulate outward. The difficulty was to
create a journal that would both express their convictions
and be financially sound. Although Lewis had interested
Sidney Schiff (the author "Stephen Hudson") in financing

1. Lewis gives an account of this incident in *Blasting and Bombardiering* (London: Eyre & Spottiswoode, 1937), pp. 270–76.
2. For Eliot's account of the trip, see "Wyndham Lewis," *Hudson
Review* 10 (Summer 1957):167–70; for Lewis's, "Early London Environment," in *T. S. Eliot: A Collection of Critical Essays,* ed. Hugh Kenner
(Englewood Cliffs, N.J.: Prentice-Hall, 1962), pp. 28–35.

the project, Schiff delayed because he thought that Lewis and Eliot would be the only first-rate contributors. Lewis then considered publishing his own art journal and received this characteristically sober advice from Eliot: "Surely the object of such a paper is to give the effect of a nucleus of intelligent independent and powerful opinion about art, and incidentally about literature and general matters." Eliot also advised that Pound be brought in as soon as possible, "since there are so few intelligent persons as it is."[3] In April 1921 Lewis brought out his cheaply printed journal *The Tyro,* which, like *Blast,* had a life of just two widely spaced issues (1921, 1922). Eliot loyally contributed three essays and a poem ("Song to the Opherian," under the pseudonym Gus Krutzsch), but he was not pleased with the results. He thought that Lewis was foolish to reproduce his own art along with that of such lesser artists as Frank Dobson and Edward Wadsworth, and rhetorically asked Lewis if he, Eliot, would think of contributing to the Sitwells' *Wheels* anthology.[4] Nor did Pound approve. Writing from Paris, he told Lewis that he was wasting time in attacking London cliques that could simply be avoided in Paris. "Can't see that *Tyro* is of interest outside Bloomsbury," Pound wrote, and added rude references to the Sitwells and Roger Fry in a verse about Paris as a place where

> Sound of —— and —— well is forgot
> And . . . .r's visage overcast with snot
> Absent from the purlieus, and in fact
> A freedom from the whole arseblarsted lot.

3. Eliot to Lewis, n.d. (before April 1921), Olin Library, Cornell University. By permission of Valerie Eliot. According to Omar S. Pound and Philip Grover's *Wyndham Lewis: A Descriptive Bibliography* (Folkestone, Kent, 1978), Schiff contributed fifty pounds toward the first issue of *The Tyro.*

4. Eliot to Lewis, n.d. (before April 1921).

He concludes this avuncular letter by telling Lewis, "You ought to get Eliot out of England somehow."[5]

Lewis and not Eliot seriously considered moving to France, but Lewis ultimately took Eliot's advice to stay in London, and probably for the reason Eliot gave him: that he would be obscured by the many clever second-raters in that art capital.[6] Pound, however, continued to urge the benefits of escaping the "hyperborean bogs" of England. Still restlessly searching for the ideal artistic environment he once glimpsed in prewar London, he moved from Paris to Italy. In a letter of 1924, Pound told Lewis that his move to Paris had rejuvenated him by fifteen years and that the move to Italy gave him another ten years of life and "more kick." This letter was prompted by a rereading of *Blast.* "We were hefty guys in them days," he wrote. "Can we kick up any more or new devilment??"[7]

By 1924 the only ready outlet for the three writers' opinions was Eliot's *Criterion,* which hardly was the place for *Blast*-style devilment. Eliot was luckier than Lewis in finding financial backing for a journal, and when the opportunity arose to publish he did not allow a troubled marriage, nervous disorders, and demanding work at his bank to discourage him. A protagonist of *The Waste Land* asks, "Shall I at least set my lands in order?"[8] By setting intellectual standards, the *Criterion* could be Eliot's contribution to order and critical awareness. He did all he could to have Pound and particularly Lewis collaborate in the new venture.

5. Pound, *Selected Letters of Ezra Pound, 1907–1941,* ed. D. D. Paige (New York: New Directions, 1971), p. 166.

6. Eliot to Lewis, n.d. (before April 1921).

7. Pound to Lewis, December 3, 1924, Olin Library, Cornell University.

8. Eliot, "The Waste Land," in *Collected Poems, 1909–1962* (New York: Harcourt Brace Jovanovich, 1963), p. 69.

He told Lewis that he wanted to keep their "association before the public mind," and requested a contribution from him, including a regular art chronicle, for every issue.[9] Eliot also editorialized in the *Criterion* on Lewis's social and philosophical criticism—such books as *The Art of Being Ruled* (1926) and *Time and Western Man* (1927)—and even hoped that the *Criterion* could become a publisher of Lewis's books. In his commentary on *The Art of Being Ruled*, Eliot saw Lewis as representative of the "dispossessed artist," who "may be driven to examining the elements in the situation— political, social, philosophical or religious—which frustrate his labour."[10] John Margolis's study of Eliot's intellectual development credits Lewis with strengthening Eliot's decision to broaden the *Criterion*'s interest in social issues.[11]

Nevertheless, by 1927 Lewis had lost confidence in Eliot's editing of his quarterly. He felt that Eliot had opened "that strange organ of Tradition" to the very forces it should be fighting. For example, though Eliot published sections from Lewis's satire of the London art world, *The Apes of God,* and told Lewis that "it is worthwhile running the *Criterion* just to publish these,"[12] at the same time he was also printing works by some of Lewis's prime satiric targets, such as Sacheverell Sitwell and Lewis's estranged patron Sidney Schiff. Lewis's basic objection was that Eliot was not really sincere about his political and social program. In *Men without Art* (1934) Lewis complained that the *Criterion*

did at one time perhaps make an effort to supply the Anglo-saxon intelligentsia with something as logically inflexible as the

9. Lewis, *The Letters of Wyndham Lewis,* ed. W. K. Rose (Norfolk, Conn.: New Directions, 1963), p. 150.

10. Eliot, "A Commentary," *Criterion* 4 (June 1926):420.

11. John Margolis, *T. S. Eliot's Intellectual Development* (Chicago: University of Chicago Press, 1972), p. 83.

12. Lewis, *Letters,* p. 140.

French periodicals of political *action* . . . but Mr. Eliot himself was not sufficiently interested. He exhibited himself as "a royalist" to an indignant whig public—he called them a lot of naughty whigs and wagged his finger and supplied *just so much* of that comedy as was welcome to brighten up the scene, but not a scrap more than was safe and comfortable.[13]

Lewis was undoubtedly oversensitive. Yet Pound felt much the same as Lewis concerning the *Criterion*'s contributors and editorial policy. Pound urged Lewis to contribute more often to the *Criterion* since it was (by default) the best outlet in England or America, and he wrote more than twenty articles and poems for it himself; but he constantly criticized Eliot for his lack of commitment, particularly on economic issues. He closed a bad-tempered letter to Eliot's quarterly with the reservation "Far be it from me to deny or affirm or in any way uncriterionisticly to commit myself . . ."[14] In *The New English Weekly,* which was now the outlet for his economic ideas, he wrote in 1934 that an analysis of many of the *Criterion*'s contributors would result in a libel action.[15] His final word on the *Criterion* is the mock elegy of 1939:

> Who killed Cock Possum?
> Who bitched his blossom?
>
> . . .
>
> "I," said ole Wyndham,
> "I bloody well skinned 'um."[16]

In their criticism of the *Criterion*'s "very 'catholic' canon," as Lewis called it, Pound and Lewis were not true to the

---

13. Lewis, *Men without Art* (London: Cassell, 1934), p. 77.
14. Pound, "Letter," *Criterion* 10 (July 1931):730.
15. Pound, "Mr. Eliot's Quandaries," *New English Weekly* 4 (March 29, 1934):559.
16. Pound, *Selected Letters,* p. 320.

Vorticist principle that the best minds, with their inevitably independent and discordant ideas, should all be put within firing range of one another. Following this principle, Eliot told Ford Madox Ford that he did not expect to agree with anyone in the *Criterion* but only to publish writers with whom it was worth disagreeing.[17] To Pound he wrote that finding a contributor of whom they both could approve would be as unlikely as seeing eye to eye with a cross-eyed man.[18] Pound and Lewis would have argued that most of the people Eliot published, such as John Middleton Murry and Herbert Read, were not worth agreeing or disagreeing with; but such an answer is a measure of their growing isolation. Both Pound and Lewis published journals (Lewis's *Enemy* and Pound's *Exile*) which were direct, personal outlets for their own ideas and were thus of much less general interest than the *Criterion*. More ominously, by the late thirties Lewis and Pound appeared, by what Pound considered a happy coincidence, in the same issue of a far more militant quarterly than Eliot's, the Fascist *British Union Quarterly*.[19] Their move toward political extremes was motivated in part by their despair of the process of open discussion that Eliot still believed in. In 1934 he told Pound that his nickname of "Rabbit" was perhaps inappropriate, for he was really a more mercurial creature, more like Marianne Moore's jerboa, which could be in two places at one time.[20] Eliot could no longer keep up with Pound's and Lewis's pace and let his two friends go their own way.

17. Eliot to Ford, February 2, 1923, Olin Library, Cornell University.
18. Eliot to Pound, April 4, 1935, Beinecke Library, Yale University.
19. Lewis, "'Left-Wings' and the C 3 Mind," *British Union Quarterly,* January/April 1937, pp. 22–34; Pound, "Demarcations," ibid., pp. 35–40.
20. Eliot to Pound, "23 Jugglio 1934," Beinecke Library, Yale University. Eliot refers to the original version of Moore's "Jerboa" in *Active Anthology,* ed. Ezra Pound (London: Faber & Faber, 1933), pp. 192–98.

The Vorticists dreamed of building a new world, but they were forced to squander their energy demolishing the old. Their efforts began diverging when they could not find a positive program to unite them. Although Eliot, Pound, and Lewis shared a commitment to order and authority, the events of the thirties subjected their political ideas to pressures that no such principle could contain.

In *For Launcelot Andrewes,* Eliot praised Lewis because he was "obviously striving courageously toward a positive theory."[21] Yet Lewis's major theoretical work, *Time and Western Man* (1927), is almost wholly destructive criticism—an attack on what Lewis calls the "time-cult." According to this Bergsonian "cult," all experience is reduced to temporal flux; even one's identity is merely a series of chronological events. In the most "positive" statement he offers, Lewis writes:

> So what we seek to stimulate, and what we give the critical outline of, is a philosophy that will be as much a *spatial-philosophy* as Bergson's is a *time-philosophy.* As much as he enjoys the sight of things "penetrating" and "merging" do we enjoy the opposite picture of them standing apart . . . much as he enjoys the "indistinct," the "qualitative," the misty, sensational and ecstatic, very much more do we value the distinct, the geometric.[22]

Lewis associates the temporal sense with the emotions and a romantic condition of becoming, and the spatial sense with the intellect and a classical state of being. (The reference to "geometric" qualities is related to T. E. Hulme's belief that

21. Eliot, *For Launcelot Andrewes* (New York: Doubleday, Doran, 1929), p. 142.
22. Lewis, *Time and Western Man* (London: Chatto & Windus, 1927), p. 443.

"geometric art" expresses a "classic" understanding of man's finite condition.) All experience should be ordered and should receive, as Pound puts it in Canto 45, "clear demarcation." The problem with Lewis's ordering, however, is that it sometimes becomes reductive. His critical schema places writers, philosophers, and scientists either "inside" (time) or "outside" (space); there is no middle position. The terms of his "critical outline" are no more related to a "positive theory" than Eliot's ambiguous statement that he considered himself "classicist in literature, royalist in politics, and Anglo-Catholic in religion."[23] His Anglo-Catholicism committed Eliot to specific beliefs but not to any political action—as Pound complained. Reacting to the religious orientation of *After Strange Gods,* Pound wrote that Eliot "implies that we need more religion, but does not specify the nature of that religion; all the implications are such as to lead the readers' minds to a fog."[24]

Pound's own "positive theory," based on Clifford Douglas's system of social credit and embellished over the years with such features as Silvio Gesell's stamp-scrip plan, was always specific if often bewildering. And his jagged technique in *The Cantos* is intended to keep his reader's mind alert and out of the "fog" by leading the reader to compare men and cultures. Pound invites us to correlate "luminous details": Sigismundo Malatesta's enormous efforts to build the Tempio (Canto 9), John Quinn's story of the "Honest Sailor's" financial success (Canto 12), the hell faced by Gaudier-Brzeska, Hulme, and Lewis in World War I (Canto 16), and Kublai Khan's invention of paper money (Canto 18). Each of these "form units," to use a term Pound used in discussing Lewis's art, both in themselves and taken to-

23. Eliot, *For Launcelot Andrewes,* p. vii.
24. Pound, "Mr. Eliot's Quandaries," p. 559.

gether, were meant to illustrate the "positive theory" that is the core of Pound's epic.

Whether ambiguous like Eliot, philosophically obscure like Lewis, or aggressively confident like Pound, each man weighed the problem of putting his ideas into action. Eliot was not so concerned with action as the other two because he thought that the intellectual should criticize and compare social theories rather than put them into practice. He was content with contributions to journals and discussion groups. But Pound and Lewis tried to take more direct action, with disastrous results for their careers.

"The great protector of the arts," Pound wrote in 1913, "is as rare as the great artist, or more so." [25] Pound discovered such a patron in John Quinn, who entered his life, as Lord Beaverbrook entered Lewis's, at a crucially early point in his artistic career. He wrote to Quinn in 1915, "If there were more like you, we should get on with our renaissance." [26] In Benito Mussolini, Pound believed that he had found not only a man sensitive to the arts (as he implies in Canto 41) but also one capable of reforming the usurious economic system that prevents the production of genuine art. The artist's duty is to recognize and welcome such a leader when he appears. By presenting such figures as Malatesta and Thomas Jefferson in *The Cantos,* Pound supposedly prepared his readers to recognize the promising qualities in such a man as Mussolini. Pound believed that he could identify vital leaders the way he once identified promising writers. He thought the "form-sense" he possessed in the Vorticist period could be applied to the political movements of the 1930s. Thus he

25. Pound, *Patria Mia,* in *Selected Prose, 1909-1965,* ed. William Cookson (New York: New Directions, 1973), p. 130.
26. Pound, *Selected Letters,* p. 51.

scolded Lewis in 1952: "Why the hell yu think that after having picked the live mind up to 1920 I shd/ suddenly have gone dead in the block perceiving live thought IN ITALY, I still don't make out."²⁷ Betrayed by this faith in his own intuition, Pound snatched at any indication that Mussolini would be the economic reformer he hoped for. Behind his desire to believe in the Fascist ruler was his conviction that only authoritarian rule could distribute economic goods fairly: "In a hide-bound Italy, fascism meant at the start DIRECT action." He thus convinced himself that "the Duce will stand not with despots and the lovers of power but with the lovers of ORDER."²⁸ In a letter to Lewis in 1939, he twisted the "E" of his signature into the rotary form of the swastika to signify his allegiance to a new kind of vortex.

Lewis also felt that only authoritarian control could remake the shell-shocked society of the postwar years and alter the economic system. When Lewis and Pound wrote a series of "Imaginary Letters" for *The Little Review*, their common theme was the intellectual obtuseness of the "herd" of common men and the appeal of art to an elite.²⁹ Eliot's judgment on the general public was also Pound's and Lewis's: "At the moments when the public's interest is

27. Pound to Lewis, 1952, Olin Library, Cornell University.
28. Pound, *Jefferson and/or Mussolini* (1935; reprinted New York: Liveright, 1970), pp. 70, 128.
29. These "Imaginary Letters" appeared in *The Little Review* in 1917. Pound decided to add his own letters to the series when Lewis's contributions, sent from France, were delayed. He apologized to Lewis for breaking into the series in an amusing letter of August 8, 1917 (Olin Library, Cornell University): "This literary rape and adultery is most underhanded and scandalous. But Mr. V[illerant] has unexpectedly come to life. . . . He is not controversing with B[urn] but discussing matters other, and of interest to his effete and over civilized organism." Pound's remark makes Mr. Villerant seem like a version of Hugh Selwyn Mauberley.

aroused, the public is never well enough informed to have the right to an opinion."[30] Proceeding from such a premise, Lewis advocated "centralized control" in *The Art of Being Ruled* (1926) and concluded that "for anglo-saxon countries as they are constituted to-day some modified form of fascism would probably be the best."[31] Like Eliot and unlike Pound, Lewis always heavily qualified his political commitments. But in his advocacy of "some modified form of fascism" he made a relatively strong statement because, like Pound, he naively believed that fascism would promote economic reform.

In 1931 Lewis wrote a book that he almost immediately regretted, *Hitler*. Lewis was careful to point out that he was an "exponent," not an "advocate," of Hitler's programs. But he was clearly impressed by Hitler's supposed economic views (rejecting but also underestimating their anti-Semetic edge) and at one point cited Eliot on social credit to explain the German position on the war debts imposed at Versailles. Pound praised Lewis's *Hitler* because it "magnificently isolated" Hitler's statement that "'the struggle against international finance and loan capital has been the most important point in the National Socialist programme.'"[32] Lewis continued to stress the distinction between "Loan-Capital" and "Creative Capital." In *Count Your Dead* (1937) he argued that "Loan-Capital" was driving Europe into war, and explained, in the primer-book style of his propaganda works, "Fascism is a revolt of the People. A revolt against debt. I am no Fascist. But I love Freedom. Also I hate

30. Quoted in Geoffrey Wagner, *Wyndham Lewis* (New Haven: Yale University Press, 1957), p. 35.

31. Lewis, *The Art of Being Ruled* (London: Chatto & Windus, 1926), pp. 367, 369.

32. Pound, *Selected Prose,* p. 299.

Usury."[33] Both Pound and Lewis believed, quite simply, that wars are caused by financial interests. Lewis wrote that "the Versailles Treaty Makers must have known that the more 'nations' you make (or break the world up into) . . . the more pickings for the Outsider."[34]

Eliot was never seduced by the notion that fascism or any other political program would necessarily reform the economic system. He reacted indignantly when Pound wrote to the *Criterion* to state some "*very simple* facts" about economics which he presumed that Eliot did not understand. Eliot replied that Pound himself introduced him to Clifford Douglas and that he and other *Criterion* writers supported Douglas's theory. As Roger Kojecky has shown, Eliot was also an adviser to the *New English Weekly,* which advocated social credit and published Ezra Pound: "The close link with *The New English Weekly* offered the prospect, never to be fulfilled, of a coherent political movement."[35] Although the movement never materialized, Eliot had certainly demonstrated his goodwill. Since Eliot could not accept extreme political movements as Pound did or tolerate them as Lewis did, he saw no way to implement such programs without betraying their liberal purpose. In answering Pound, Eliot argued for "the priority of ethics over politics."[36]

All three men approached these issues as, to use Eliot's phrase for Lewis, "dispossessed artists." As artists, Pound and Eliot would have agreed with Lewis's justification of a

33. Lewis, *Count Your Dead: They Are Alive! or A New War in the Making* (1937; reprinted New York: Gordon Press, 1972), p. 276.
34. Lewis, *Hitler* (London: Chatto & Windus, 1931), p. 76.
35. Roger Kojecky, *T. S. Eliot's Social Criticism* (New York: Farrar, Strauss & Giroux, 1971), p. 81.
36. Pound's letter appears in *Criterion* 13 (October 1933):128; Eliot's reply is in the "Commentary" of the same issue, p. 119.

strong central authority: "to get some sort of peace to enable us to work, we should naturally seek the most powerful and stable authority that can be devised."[37] "A VORTICIST KING! WHY NOT?" Lewis had shouted in *Blast,* and in the 1919 *Caliph's Design* he dreamed of the enlightened monarch who enriched his subjects' lives by transforming their visual environment. In *The Tyro,* Lewis continued to hope that new styles of architecture would give heart to the common man:

> A man might be unacquainted with the very existence of a certain movement in art, and yet his life would be modified directly if the street he walked down took a certain shape. . . . Its forms and colours would have a tonic or a debilitating effect on him. . . . The painting, sculpture and general design of today, such as can be included in the movement we support, aims at nothing short of a physical reconstructing . . . of the visible part of the world.[38]

In admiring the above passage, Stephen Spender finds that it reflects one of the major qualities of modern art: "the invention through art of a *pattern of hope,* influencing society." Lewis and the Vorticists believed, to use Spender's words, "that modern art might transform the contemporary environment, and hence, by pacifying and ennobling its inhabitants, revolutionize the world."[39] Unfortunately, the Vorticist Caliph was an artist's dream, the Fascist dictator a political reality.

The Vortex does not reveal the development of an intellectual or social program, but rather what Spender calls a

---

37. Lewis, *Art of Being Ruled,* pp. 369–70.

38. Quoted in Stephen Spender, *The Struggle of the Modern* (London: Hamish Hamilton, 1963), pp. 85–86.

39. Ibid., pp. 83–84.

"pattern of hope." Modern literature was not born in despair after World War I, but before the war, in the hope of transfiguring every element of life through a new renaissance. By the middle thirties this hope was no longer viable. Pound alone kept pushing for a revival of the Vorticist group, even suggesting a new issue of *Blast* to Lewis as late as 1936. His support of Lewis continued long after Lewis had any desire for it—praising *Hitler,* for example, after Lewis had disowned the book.

Pound's fate during and especially after World War II, when he was imprisoned for treason and then declared mentally unfit to stand trial, is well known, indeed notorious. Lewis's fate was not so severe but harsh nonetheless. His unpopular political writings, especially *Hitler,* put his entire literary career under a cloud, and a series of illnesses left him deeply in debt. One of his major efforts as a novelist, *The Revenge for Love* (1937), was written, published, and reviewed in an atmosphere that George Orwell called "completely ruinous to the novel."[40] Lewis was still active as a painter. He painted perhaps his greatest portrait in 1937 when Pound sat for him during a brief visit to England, and he received valuable publicity when Augustus John resigned in protest against the Royal Academy's refusal to exhibit Lewis's magnificent 1938 portrait of T. S. Eliot and Winston Churchill praised the Academy's defense of its academic standards.[41] But the prewar market was barren for even the best of artists, and in 1939 Lewis and his wife sailed to America, where he was promised some portrait commissions. In New York he met Pound, who came from Italy for a one-man effort to prevent the approaching war. He was as eager

40. George Orwell, *Collected Essays* (London: Secker & Warburg, 1961), p. 148.
41. See Lewis, *Letters,* pp. 250–57.

as ever to help Lewis through impractical schemes, such as arranging for Lewis to paint a senator's portrait. Neither of them had a successful stay in America and both were about to become aliens under wartime conditions. Lewis planned on a quick return to England, but the war stranded him in Canada. His lonely, impoverished years in Toronto became the subject of his greatest novel, *Self Condemned* (1954).

Lewis's novel is representative of the kind of introspection all three writers underwent as a result of World War II. The spirit of both *Self Condemned* and *The Pisan Cantos* is reflected in the following great lines from Eliot's "Little Gidding," in which he lists the "gifts reserved for age":

> the conscious impotence of rage
> At human folly, and the laceration
> Of laughter at what ceases to amuse.
> And last, the rending pain of re-enactment
> Of all that you have done, and been; the shame
> Of motives late revealed, and the awareness
> Of things ill done and done to others' harm. . . .[42]

Although the theme of *Self Condemned* is in these lines, the novel nowhere states it with this precision. Sometimes it is hard to tell whether Lewis is justifying or condemning his protagonist. The novel's greatness lies in what Eliot called its tone of "almost unbearable spiritual agony."[43]

The protagonist of *Self Condemned,* René Harding, resigns his chair of history shortly before World War II breaks out because he believes that his subject as it is presently taught encourages the war psychosis. He claims that historians dignify the warmakers and systematically

42. T. S. Eliot, *Collected Poems, 1909–1963* (New York: Harcourt Brace Jovanovich, 1963), p. 204.
43. Eliot, "A Note on *Monstre Gai,*" *Hudson Review* 7 (Winter 1955):524.

ignore the economic causes of war. Now that a second war is blacking out his hopes for a new enlightenment, he chooses to go to Canada and avoid the "foully comic" drama the war will bring to England. In Canada, poverty and intellectual isolation transform his rebelliousness and courage into despair. He once believed that the period between 1914 and 1918—years of "creative inventiveness" as well as of "criminal destructiveness"—could have been the "giant backcloth for a New Year One" and "twentieth-century rebirth." René now believes that the brief periods of civilization that humanity has known were the exceptions to the rule of animal brutality and greed. Western civilization is dying: "He estimated that we were perhaps rather more than half-way across that, in geological terms, infinitely brief era of 'enlightenment.'"[44] This passage echoes the conclusion of one of Lewis's favorite books of the post–World War I period, Julien Benda's *La Trahison des clercs* (1927). But in this post–World War II novel such ideas are put in a new and harsher light. In René Harding they lead to a contempt of the masses, who are producing what he considers to be the new dark ages. Four years before *Self Condemned* was published, Lewis admitted in *The Art of Being Ruled* that "a tincture of intolerance here and there regarding the backward, slothful, obstructive majority—'homo stultus'—is present."[45] This intolerance, in an extreme form, corrupts René. One senses the novel's "spiritual agony" as Lewis traces this corruption in his autobiographical protagonist. As René loses his idealism and writes historical studies that despair of human progress, he ironically becomes a famous author; but he "no longer even believed in his theories of a new approach to History . . . for him it had all frozen into a freak anti-

44. Lewis, *Self Condemned* (London: Methuen, 1954), pp. 84, 211.
45. Lewis, *Rude Assignment* (London: Hutchinson, 1950), p. 188.

historical museum, of which he was the Keeper, containing many libellous wax-works of famous kings and queens. He carried on mechanically with what the bright, rushing, idealistic mind of another man had begun."[46] By the novel's conclusion, his misanthropy has turned him into a "glacial shell of a man."

Self Condemned is not only an autobiographical novel; it is also a meditation on Ezra Pound's career, the meaning of which is so like that of Lewis's that the double reference of René's character is perfectly congruent. External signs of Pound's presence in the work may be seen in the Hardings' London flat, which is based on Lewis's memories of Pound's triangular flat in Kensington, where Lewis first met T. S. Eliot. René's physical appearance is based on Pound's: his "eyes were at the cat-like angle, glittering out of a slit," as in Lewis's drawings of Pound in 1920, and he likes "to assume half-recumbent attitudes," as in Lewis's 1937 portrait of Pound.[47] From this perspective, one can see that the "anti-historical museum" that René creates refers to *The Cantos*. René's method of writing history, in which economics is stressed and strong moral stands are taken, duplicates Pound's method in creating his epic, or "poem containing history." Lewis's implied judgment is that the method conceived by the "bright, rushing, idealistic mind" of the poet of *A Draft of XXX Cantos* becomes the formula "mechanically" continued by the author of the *Rock-Drill* cantos.

René's spiritual fate is not Pound's. But just as René's character reflects Lewis's impatience with the common man, so does it reflect Pound's. In 1946 Lewis responded to

46. Lewis, *Self Condemned*, p. 400.
47. Ibid., p. 7. See also Hugh Kenner, *The Pound Era* (Berkeley and Los Angeles: University of California Press, 1971), p. 501.

Pound's criticism of America by telling him that he admired the "simple pleasant people (butchers, bakers and candlestick makers) whom you would despise."[48] The tragic characteristic in René that is particularly related to Pound, however, is the "perfectionism" that underlies his anger and contempt. Lewis in 1949 praised Pound as a "professional" who expected perfection in art. The dark side of this quality, however, is that "he demands *perfection* in action, as well as in art. He even appears to expect perfection, or what he understands as such, in the world of politics."[49] Early in *Self Condemned,* René is indignant when his closest friend refers to him as an "implacable perfectionist" who opposes the "inventive and creative few" to the "uncreative majority." He protests that he realizes that "'life is a half-way house, a place of obligatory compromise.'"[50] But exile and war drive him to repudiate "the compromise of normal living." As in the case of Ezra Pound, an increasing "violence of thought" accompanies growing "mental instability" and results in "excesses of virulent expression."[51] These excesses are the tragic counterparts of his idealism and passion for the truth. Like René, Pound in Lewis's eyes suffered a "tragic fracture of the personality." Lewis restated this theme in the 1954 "Doppelgänger: A Story," in which Pound's character is split into two personae, one wise and one foolish.[52] This doubling of personalities expresses Lewis's bewilderment concerning his friend's combination of greatness and triviality. Lewis

48. Lewis, *Letters,* p. 398.
49. Lewis, "Ezra Pound," in *Ezra Pound: A Collection of Essays,* ed. Peter Russell (New York: Haskell House, 1968), p. 263. This essay was originally published in the *Quarterly Review of Literature* in 1949.
50. Lewis, *Self Condemned,* p. 96.
51. Ibid., p. 356.
52. Lewis, "Doppelgänger: A Story," *Encounter* 2 (January 1954):23–33.

would have agreed with Charles Olson's judgment that Pound is "the tragic Double of our day."[53]

In the early fifties Pound's fate seemed all the darker when contrasted, as it was in Lewis's mind, with the triumphal climax of Eliot's career. In an essay written to commemorate Eliot's sixtieth birthday, an exercise that almost mischievously turned into a tribute to Pound rather than to Eliot, Lewis noted that while Eliot was "dwelling in the bland atmosphere of general approbation," Pound was "confined in a criminal asylum in America." He wondered what could draw Eliot "up into so brilliantly sunlit a position" and Pound "down into such portentous shadows." Lewis concluded pessimistically, "For me I think the question tends to take no count of the climb up into the sun, but only the problem of what keeps anybody . . . out of a madhouse."[54] Lewis felt that Pound's wrongheaded but passionately held political stands gave his career greater integrity than Eliot's, and therefore less worldly success. Such integrity exacts a price. When Pound praised the satiric anger he found in Lewis's 1914 *Timon* designs, he warned that "a man with [Lewis's] kind of intelligence is bound to be always crashing and opposing and breaking. You cannot be as intelligent, in that sort of way, without being prey to the furies."[55] Although his insight into Lewis's character was acute, this comment is more tragically relevant to his own career.

"Yuss, my beamish buckO!" Pound wrote after reading *Self Condemned,* "this ɪᴢ some book," and he added in a

53. *Charles Olson and Ezra Pound : An Encounter at St. Elizabeths,* ed. Catherine Seelye (New York: Viking Press, 1975), p. xvi.
54. Lewis, "Early London Environment," in *T. S. Eliot: A Collection of Critical Essays* (Englewood Cliffs, N.J.: Prentice-Hall, 1962), p. 28. This essay was originally published in 1948.
55. Pound, "Edward Wadsworth, Vorticist," *Egoist* 1 (August 15, 1914):306.

56

later letter from St. Elizabeths, the mental hospital in which he was then confined, "Shd / git yu the Nobble."[56] He seemed to have some grasp of Lewis's criticism of him, for he wrote to Lewis of *Self Condemned*'s "tenzone with Cantares," though without developing the nature of this conflict between the novel and *The Cantos.*[57] The "tenzone" between the two men was strong throughout the St. Elizabeths period. Pound sent long letters of detailed notes concerning such works as Lewis's *Rude Assignment* and on his book about the political pressures felt by the modern artist, *The Writer and the Absolute.* He ridiculed Lewis for his views on World War II and lectured him on the way British foreign policy drove Mussolini into alliance with Hitler. Pound urged Lewis to contribute to the journals he supported, even brief notes that would at least establish a Pound-Lewis connection, and recommended to him a series of books that ranged from Greek philosophy to modern economics. Lewis replied that he could not handle Pound's book list and mildly suggested that Eliot had more leisure for such reading.[58]

Eliot was often a subject of the Pound-Lewis correspondence. One exchange reflected their misgivings over Eliot's Nobel Prize, with each man strenuously asserting that he felt no envy; but both Pound and Lewis hoped that now that Eliot had reached the summit of recognition, he would abandon his caution as a publisher and critic. A focus of Lewis's annoyance with Eliot as a publisher was what Lewis felt to be his reluctance to publish Pound's letters. Lewis prodded Eliot tirelessly on this issue and assisted D. D. Paige's editing of the letters because he was convinced that

56. Pound to Lewis, November 19, 1954, and December 6, 1954, Olin Library, Cornell University.
57. Pound to Lewis, December 6, 1954.
58. Lewis, *Letters,* p. 453.

publication would increase respect for Pound and thus help to free him from St. Elizabeths. Eliot was just as energetic as Lewis in working for Pound's release, however, and of course his fame made him far more effective.

From the days of the *Criterion,* when Eliot drew no salary himself in order to help pay his contributors, Eliot was a generous supporter of his friends, particularly Pound and Lewis. He also made sure that his publishing firm printed their works. Although Pound complained that Eliot would publish only the "approximately Xtn. parts" of his work, Eliot told Pound that Faber would always have a standing order for *The Cantos.*[59] He also supported Lewis's painting by sitting for a second portrait in 1949. When Lewis was unable to sell the portrait, Eliot bought it himself.[60] The portrait was painted even as Lewis was steadily losing his sight. Loans from Eliot allowed Lewis to travel to Sweden and Switzerland for medical advice, but the brain tumor that was causing the blindness could not be surgically removed without risk to his mental faculties. In the darkness that soon came to Lewis, Eliot was again a support as he read proof for Lewis's trilogy *The Human Age.*

Pound kept the idea of the Vortex alive. In 1955 he complained to Lewis about their lack of concerted action: "WORTEXXX, gorrdammit, some convergence."[61] *The Pisan Cantos* show that his thoughts kept returning to pre–World War I England, as in his memories of the "British Museum era" in Canto 80; and in Canto 78 he asserted that Lewis and Gaudier (the latter's pronunciation of the word "vortex" is echoed in Pound's "WORTEXXX") were still vital influences:

59. Eliot to Pound, January 16, 1934, Beinecke Library, Yale University.
60. See my "Wyndham Lewis's Portraits of T. S. Eliot," *T. S. Eliot Newsletter* 1 (Spring 1974):4.
61. Pound to Lewis, January 20, 1955, Olin Library, Cornell University.

in whom are the voices, keeping hand on the reins
Gaudier's word not blacked out
      nor old Hulme's, nor Wyndham's . . .

Such moments of assertion are not typical of *The Pisan Cantos*. Pound reveals the kind of remorse Lewis expresses in *Self Condemned*. Although no more consistently than Lewis, he writes of a man self-condemned, "that had been a hard man in some ways,"

      j'ai eu pitié des autres
probablement pas assez, and at moments that suited
      [my own convenience. . . .

These self-doubts were not so common to Pound during his St. Elizabeths period. He kept driving at his economic theories, and Lewis's description of Pound's "rock-drill action . . . he blasts away tirelessly, prodding and coaxing," delighted him and inspired the title for *Section: Rock-Drill de los Cantares* (1955).[62] His ambitions were still at a Vorticist height of energy in the 1959 *Thrones,* which he described as "an attempt to move out from egoism and to establish some definition of an order possible or at any rate conceivable on earth."[63] They declined only when he was in his eighties. In *Drafts & Fragments* (1969) he admitted his failures ("that I lost my center / fighting the world"), but in lines of poetry that are themselves a triumph:

      I have brought the great ball of crystal;
          who can lift it?

62. Lewis, "The Rock Drill" (1951), in *Ezra Pound: Perspectives,* ed. Noel Stock (Chicago: Henry Regnery, 1965), p. 198.
63. Donald Hall, "Ezra Pound: An Interview," *Paris Review* 28 (Summer/Fall, 1962):49.

> Can you enter the great acorn of light?
> But the beauty is not the madness
> Tho' my errors and wrecks lie about me.[64]

The depression Pound fell into after his release from St. Elizabeths in 1958 was deepened by memories of Eliot and Lewis. Pound's daughter Mary de Rachewiltz recalls that after her father returned to Italy "he was plagued by all kinds of remorse. Mr. Eliot was one: 'I should have listened to the Possum.' And we all had to read *After Strange Gods*. I wrote to Mr. Eliot begging him to come and see Babbo. He sent a birthday telegram saying: 'You are the greatest poet alive and I owe everything to you'—or words to that effect."[65] The telegram is in the Yale University Pound collection, together with the tactful and compassionate letter that followed it to apologize for the necessary brevity of the cable. Eliot's letter explains that *After Strange Gods* is a poor book because of the financial and personal strains under which it was written. He tells his friend that he knows, having suffered similar states of doubt and despair, how little his praise of Pound's greatness as a poet may mean. Yet he again asserts that Pound's achievement as a poet is the greatest in their lifetimes.[66]

Wyndham Lewis's death in 1957 inspired the most beautiful poem in *Drafts & Fragments*, "From Canto CXV," which is Pound's elegy for Lewis. The opening lines contrast Lewis's intellectual energy with current decadence:

64. Pound, *Drafts & Fragments* (New York: New Directions, 1969), pp. 795–96.

65. Mary de Rachewiltz, *Discretions* (Boston: Little, Brown, 1971), p. 306.

66. Eliot to Pound, December 28, 1959, Bienecke Library, Yale University.

> The scientists are in terror
> and the European mind stops
> Wyndham Lewis chose blindness
> rather than have his mind stop.[67]

In this heroic image of Lewis, Pound refers to Lewis's decision not to risk an operation that might save his sight but darken his mind. Lewis's blindness relates him in a figurative sense to the writers Pound describes in Canto 110: "all the resisters blacked out." Yet Pound is still critical of what he considers Lewis's failure to achieve "convergence." In a reference to his friend's economic naiveté he writes in Canto 102: "But the lot of 'em, Yeats, Possum, Old Wyndham / had no ground to stand on." In Canto 115, he comments wearily on the vanity of Lewis's time-space categories and on any intellectual system that tries to impose an unfounded order upon experience: "Time, space, / neither life nor death is the answer."

Pound had the grandest designs for the new culture the Vorticists hoped to build, and he was consequently more painfully disillusioned than Lewis and certainly more than the naturally skeptical Eliot. Lewis wrote in 1937 of the generation he called the "men of 1914": "We are the first men of a Future that has not materialized. We belong to a 'great age' that has not 'come off.'"[68] Similarly, Eliot wrote

67. Pound, *Drafts & Fragments,* p. 794. An early version of this fragment is less dramatic but more accurate on the subject of Lewis's blindness:

> Preferring blindness to chance of having his mind stop, when European
> mind does stop and *has* stopped.

Lewis certainly did not "choose" blindness. The early version is quoted in Ronald Duncan, *How to Make Enemies* (London: Rupert Hart-Davis, 1968), p. 330.
68. Lewis, *Blasting and Bombardiering,* p. 258.

in the final issue of the *Criterion* that in 1926 he "began slowly to realize that the intellectual and artistic output of the previous seven years had been rather the last efforts of an old world, than the first struggles of a new."[69]

Yet none of these three "dispossessed artists" thought that their personal struggles were wasted. In an implicit comment on *The Caliph's Design,* Lewis wrote that the foundation of our "proposed City-Beautiful turned out to be not rock, as we had naively supposed, but some disintegrating living substance."[70] He added, however, that one can build "in one's dreams," anticipating Pound's assertion in *The Pisan Cantos* that his ideal "city of Dioce" was now "in the mind indestructable." Eliot meant the same when he wrote of the "Idea" of a Christian society. The ultimate form of the vortex is a "pattern of hope," such as Pound describes in Canto 116:

> to affirm the gold thread in the pattern. . . .
> A little light, like a rushlight
> to lead back to splendour.

69. Eliot, "Last Words," *Criterion* 18 (January 1939):271.
70. Lewis, *The Mysterious Mr. Bull* (1938), quoted in D. G. Bridson, *The Filibuster: A Study of the Political Ideas of Wyndham Lewis* (London: Cassell, 1972), p. 206.

3

"Gaudier-Brzeska Vortex"

Will and consciousness are our
VORTEX.
—Henri Gaudier, *Blast*

Henri Gaudier-Brzeska's death in World War I at the
age of twenty-three haunted Pound and Lewis throughout
their careers. Pound told Lewis that his "serious curiosity"
about politics and economics began at Gaudier's death, and
Charles Olson reports that Pound was still grieving for Gaudier in the late 1940s: "It is as though Pound has never got over
it . . . all his turn since has been revenge for the boy's
death."[1] Lewis's reaction to Gaudier's death was just as
bitter: "[Gaudier] was so preternaturally *alive* . . . that I
began my lesson then: a lesson of hatred for this soulless
machine, of big-wig money government."[2] Lewis illustrated
this lesson in his 1937 novel *The Revenge for Love,* in which
the artist Victor Stamp, a character inspired in part by
Gaudier, becomes involved in a political intrigue that takes
his life.

The dramatic events of Gaudier's life as well as its tragic
end have obscured his artistic career. Instead of evaluating
his considerable achievements, his critics too often lament
the loss of works that Gaudier might have sculpted had he

1. Ezra Pound to Wyndham Lewis, January 25, 1949, Olin Library,
Cornell University; *Charles Olson and Ezra Pound: An Encounter at St.
Elizabeths,* ed. Catherine Seelye (New York: Viking Press, 1975), p. 45.
2. Lewis, *Blasting and Bombardiering* (London: Eyre & Spottiswoode,
1937), pp. 114–15.

lived. A second obstacle to an evaluation of his career is the controversy aroused by the Vorticist movement. Gaudier's critics, especially the early ones, have been drawn into debating the merits of Vorticism and whether Gaudier was truly a Vorticist. He was undeniably one of the 1914 Vorticists, but his aesthetics was less doctrinaire than were those of Lewis and the other Vorticists. A mark of Gaudier's genius is that he achieved Vorticism's goals, not as Lewis and Pound formulated them in 1914 but rather as they understood them years later.

Pound's *Gaudier-Brzeska: A Memoir* (1916) is in part responsible for the distracting question of whether Gaudier was actually a Vorticist. Pound's claims for Gaudier's Vorticism were so aggressive that his book at first did as much harm as good for the understanding of Gaudier's art. One can only imagine what Gaudier's reaction to Pound's memoir might have been; the case of the composer George Antheil, however, suggests one possibility. When Pound met Antheil in Paris in 1923, the American composer-pianist was only twenty-three years old—the age at which Gaudier had died—and already a brilliant recitalist and promising avant-garde composer. He must have seemed to Pound the Vorticist composer that the rebels once hoped for when they misspelled the names of Schönberg and Scriabin in announcing lecturers at the Rebel Art Centre. Antheil's temperament was certainly Vorticist. He attributed his coolness during demonstrations against the modern music he played at his concerts to the small .32-caliber automatic pistol he wore under his tuxedo. To quiet a potentially riotous audience in Budapest, he brandished his weapon and then, as he describes it, "placed it on the front desk of my Steinway and proceeded with my concert. Every note was heard."[3]

3. George Antheil, *Bad Boy of Music* (London: Hurst & Blackett, 1947), p. 11.

His aesthetics was also Vorticist in spirit. His notorious *Ballet mécanique* was scored for electric bells, automobile horns, airplane propellers, and pieces of tin and steel. Pound introduced himself to this prodigy as an "expert in genius," borrowed his jottings on music theory, and some months later returned with the proofs of *Antheil and the Theory of Harmony.* Antheil was pleased with the book at first but later regretted the problems it caused:

> Ezra's flamboyant book, couched in language calculated to antagonize everyone first by its ridiculous praise, then by its vicious criticism of everybody else, did me no good whatsoever; on the contrary, it sowed the most active distaste for the very mention of the name Antheil among many contemporary critics, prejudiced them before thay had even so much as heard a note of mine. Nobody could have been a tenth as good as Ezra made me.[4]

Antheil's musical fireworks soon burned out. His compositions became more conservative, and Pound walked out in disapproval at a performance of Antheil's "classical" Second Symphony.

Although, as we shall see, Gaudier did not always approve of Pound's judgments, and might have been as disturbed by *Gaudier-Brzeska* as the composer was by *Antheil,* his much closer friendship with Pound could have prevented serious misunderstandings. Even before Pound met Gaudier, he encouraged him by purchasing his sculptures, and Pound's final act of generosity toward Gaudier was to lend him the money to return to France at the outbreak of war. After Gaudier's death, Pound became not only his biographer but also executor of his works. Yet there were also personal strains in their relationship. Our knowledge of their friendship rests largely on Pound's own *Gaudier-Brzeska.* Noel

4. Ibid., p. 98.

Stock's *Life of Ezra Pound* and Hugh Kenner's *Pound Era* portray the friendship in Pound's terms, with Pound appearing as Gaudier's generous patron and critic. The view of the Pound-Gaudier relationship presented by one of Gaudier's close friends, Horace Brodzky, is generally ignored. Brodzky felt (as did Jacob Epstein) that Pound's *Gaudier-Brzeska* was too literary a treatment of the sculptor. He complained in his own book, *Henri Gaudier-Brzeska,* that Pound "had stuffed his book with his own theories, which had little application to [Gaudier]."[5] Brodzky thought that there never was a sincere friendship between the poet and the sculptor and that Gaudier's sculpting of Pound in the form of a giant phallus (the *Hieratic Head of Ezra Pound*) was done "by way of disapproval and in contempt of Pound."[6] Since Brodzky himself disapproved of Pound's avant-garde influence on Gaudier, one should be suspicious of his claims. On the other hand, Brodzky knew Gaudier far longer and more intimately than did Pound.

Aside from Pound and Brodzky, the principal source for our knowledge of Henri Gaudier's life is H. S. Ede's *Savage Messiah* (1931). This biography, like the Ken Russell film of the same title based upon it, is essentially the story of Gaudier's unhappy love for Sophie Brzeska. They met in Paris in 1910, when Gaudier was eighteen and Sophie Brzeska thirty-eight. Brzeska had fled from her unhappy home in Poland to become a nursemaid and governess in a series of families, including some in America. She met Gaudier after a lover had deserted her in Germany and after

5. Horace Brodzky, *Henri Gaudier-Brzeska, 1891-1915* (London: Faber & Faber, 1933), pp. 99-100. Jacob Epstein said that Gaudier's "first appraisers are distinguished by their knowledge of literature rather than by their knowledge of art" (*Let There Be Sculpture* [New York: G. P. Putnam's Sons, 1940], p. 36).

6. Brodzky, *Henri Gaudier-Brzeska,* p. 60.

what she took to be a final rejection by her family. Possessed by what she calls in her diary *"l'inséparable idée du suicide,"* she had an intensity that attracted the young artist. Gaudier told a friend that

> she has an entirely independent nature, is an anarchist— simply and naturally, has a beauty *à la* Baudelaire—and might have stepped out of *Fleurs du Mal.* She is lithe and simple, with a feline carriage and enigmatic face, the fine character of which reflects her most intimate thoughts—planes combining in the most surprising manner, impressions of age and of youth in alarming contrast.[7]

Although Henri saw her through a haze of literary and sculptural impressions, his four years with her proved the genuineness of his devotion. He hoped that she would one day return the physical passion he felt for her. But from the first she saw Gaudier as a son she could protect and educate, and her firmness in this role is indicated by the altered heading of her diary: from *"Séjour à Londres"* to *"A mon fils adoptif."* As Rebecca West writes, "The young and hopeful boy made a gesture of the deepest significance by assuming the rough and unpronounceable name of this veteran in tragedy."[8] It is as if Gaudier prematurely took on the tragic experience of a lifetime by becoming Gaudier-Brzeska.

After returning from trips to England and Germany in 1910, Gaudier studied anatomy in Paris. He was a brilliant student and twice went to England on scholarships. Like the young James Joyce two years earlier, he followed his own

7. H. S. Ede, *Savage Messiah* (1931; reprinted Bedford: Gordon Fraser, 1971), p. 7.

8. Rebecca West, "The Pursuit of Misery as a Fine Art," *Daily Telegraph,* May 1, 1931. I am quoting from a clipping in H. S. Ede's collection.

course of study in Paris by reading at the Bibliothèque Sainte-Geneviève. He met Sophie Brzeska there while she was reading German literature. They visited Gaudier's family home in Orléans (his father was a wood carver), where they caused a scandal among the local farmers, and then decided to use Brzeska's small savings to travel to England. Gaudier wanted to avoid serving in the French army, which he called the "slaughterers of the Arabs," and thought he could easily find work in England. Once in London, lonely and poor, they regretted their impulsive flight from France. Gaudier finally found a job answering foreign correspondence for a business firm and began to make friends, but Brzeska always felt alien and vented her frustrations in her diary.

H. S. Ede might have clarified the Pound-Gaudier relationship because the source for his book was Sophie's 1910–14 diary. The remarkable intensity of *Savage Messiah,* however, derives from its concentration upon Henri and Sophie's love to the point where less dramatic aspects of their lives are minimized. Ede's biography therefore gives the impression that Sophie's diary had little to record about Pound. The diary itself contradicts this impression. Ezra Pound plays a major and almost sinister role in Sophie Brzeska's account of her life with Henri Gaudier.

Brzeska's diary for the years 1910–14 has been unavailable for many years.[9] When W. B. Yeats read Ede's *Savage Messiah,* he at first doubted that the diary existed. Yeats finally decided that it did exist and shrewdly wondered "if [Brzeska] was not after all a great novelist."[10] Its vivid dialogue and descriptions do give the diary novelistic quali-

9. H. S. Ede has recently made the diary available at Kettle's Yard, University of Cambridge. The diary for the years 1915–22 is at the University of Essex.

10. Yeats, *The Letters of W. B. Yeats,* ed. Allen Wade (London: Rupert Hart-Davis, 1954), p. 782.

ties. These qualities produce the sense of direct involvement in Brzeska's life that Yeats admired in *Savage Messiah.* She apparently planned to use her diary as a source for a novel. The pre-1915 diary is headed "Notes [*Détails*] for Matka," and *Matka* is the autobiographical work she hoped to write but barely started. Yeats also noted an essential quality of Sophie Brzeska which we must keep in mind in order to interpret her journal accurately. In describing Brzeska, Yeats tells Olivia Shakespear: "I think she must have had [sexual] experience, have thought herself wronged perhaps and developed an hysterical dread of experience, and that [Gaudier] must have desired her. . . . An hysterical woman has sometimes a strong fascination, she is a whirlpool—such a problem to herself that everybody within reach is drawn in. She rouses an ungovernable pity and pity soon touches the senses."[11] A reading of the diary bears out Yeats's insight. Her suffering is so compelling that one has to guard against accepting uncritically her judgments of people, such as Ezra Pound and Jacob Epstein, who came between her and Gaudier. Epstein himself said that Brzeska "was intensely and morbidly jealous of all [Gaudier's] friends."[12]

With these cautions in mind, one can examine Sophie Brzeska's version of Gaudier's relationship with Ezra Pound, in which Pound will of course not appear as a generous friend and patron.[13] Her first mention of Pound appears in a

11. Ibid., p. 783.
12. Jacob Epstein to Arnold L. Haskell, in *The Sculptor Speaks* (London: William Heinemann, 1931), p. 134. Sophie Brzeska's dislike of Epstein and of Gaudier's other Jewish friends was aggravated by an anti-Semitism that was a poisonous aspect of her persecution complex.
13. I was assisted in my translations from Sophie Brzeska's French by M. Bonner Mitchell, professor of Romance languages, University of Missouri at Columbia. I sympathize with H. S. Ede's statement that "usually the Diary is too diffuse, and too personal to Miss Brzeska, to allow of a direct translation" (*Savage Messiah,* p. 7).

conversation with Gaudier about abstract and realistic art. To Brzeska's displeasure, Gaudier says that he is now an abstract artist, and he compares his work with the poetry of Ezra Pound. Brzeska replies that Pound's poetry "'doesn't appeal to me very much—in its ideas or in its form.'" Gaudier replies, "'There aren't any ideas in the poetry of Ezra Pound . . . There are only emotions that are released from it.'" She asks Gaudier to explain these emotions to her and adds, no doubt ironically, "'I am very humble and want to learn from you.'" Gaudier then ends the exchange: "'Well, if you can't understand it, I can't explain it to you. I just feel it, and there's an end of it.'"[14]

Gaudier seems to have admired Pound's poetry before he knew him personally. They met shortly after Pound bought two of Gaudier's sculptures for fifteen pounds. (Brzeska thought this price far too low.) John Cournos writes that he brought the two artists together in Pound's room at Church Walk, Kensington.[15] They had met briefly, however, at an exhibition in Albert Hall, when Gaudier-Brzeska suddenly appeared to correct Pound's pronunciation of his hyphenated name and then "disappeared like a Greek god in a vision."[16] Gaudier was greatly heartened when Cournos told him that the poet he so respected would purchase his works, and Pound's reaction to the new friendship was equally enthusiastic. He wrote to William Carlos Williams that Gaudier "is

14. The last two sentences quoted are from Ede's translation in *Savage Messiah,* p. 151. Since this is Ede's only quotation from the scene, he makes Gaudier seem more abrupt than he is in Brzeska's version. Ede says that Gaudier specifically compared his *Red Stone Dancer* to Pound's poetry.

15. John Cournos, *Autobiography* (New York: G. P. Putnam's Sons, 1935), p. 260.

16. Ezra Pound, *Gaudier-Brzeska: A Memoir* (New York: New Directions, 1970), p. 44.

the only person with whom I can really be 'Altaforce' . . . We are getting our little gang after five years of waiting."[17]

The most interesting episode in Brzeska's account of their meetings with Pound occurs when Pound takes them to dinner at the Café Royal. Brzeska's wonderfully detailed description of their conversation convinces one that she is describing events as accurately as she can. Throughout the diary, her record of the most hostile and petty exchanges between herself and Gaudier also suggests her devotion to accuracy. On the night of the dinner, she and Gaudier met Pound at his flat. Her description of her first meeting with Pound gives an impressive picture of him (in the following scene, I assume that Pound has called the Gaudier-Brzeskas into his bedroom, where he had been reading or writing): "When we went into his bedroom a man with kinky blond hair—and a little pointed beard—his nose ornamented with pince-nez glasses, rose to greet us. He seemed rather pleasant and unaffected to me with his long dressing gown à la Balzac. Did he forget in his 'abstraction' that an unknown woman was to see him?"

Despite Pound's evident friendliness, Brzeska fears that Pound's friend John Cournos has prejudiced the poet against her. She is also nervous because she has argued with Gaudier before arriving at Pound's flat: "War was declared between us." At the Café Royal, Brzeska feels increasingly inadequate as she listens to Pound's theories of art. Since her English is still a bit weak, she finds it difficult to follow what she calls the "torrent of Pound's words—pronounced with a nervous vivacity." But she is roused to challenge Pound when he begins to speak of "abstract" art. She asks Pound to explain

17. Pound, *Selected Letters of Ezra Pound, 1907–1941,* ed. D. D. Paige (New York: New Directions, 1971), p. 27.

his distinction between the feelings and the emotions. She cannot entirely follow Pound's answer. If his explanation resembles the vertiginous distinctions that T. S. Eliot makes in "Tradition and the Individual Talent" among "floating feelings," "personal emotions," and the "art emotion," her confusion is understandable quite apart from the language difficulty.[18] But she does manage to record Pound's basic distinction between emotions and feelings, which helps one understand what Gaudier meant by "abstract" art. Pound explains that feelings refer to the responses of individuals while emotions are sensations that emanate from a poem or other work of art. If abstract art expresses art emotions rather than the feelings of individuals, it is "abstract" in the sense of being impersonal. Such works as the primitive art that Gaudier admired are complete in themselves and not expressive of the artist's personality. Pound and Gaudier are here still a long way from a theory of "abstract" art as nonrepresentative art.

Annoyed by Brzeska's failure to understand avant-garde art, Gaudier says that women should not dabble in art. Pound agrees and asks, "'Why do [women] trouble themselves about these matters—why worry about their battle for emancipation—since they're strong enough to dominate us.'" When Brzeska asks if he is speaking seriously, Pound answers, "'Perfectly. And I believe it.'" Brzeska says that she is not interested in dominance. Pound replies, "'I shall tell you the sort [of woman] I admire very much,'" and tells the story of Marozia, the wife of three powerful Italian rulers, about whom he once planned to write an epic.[19]

18. For the background of this distinction, see Glen S. Burne, *Remy de Gourmont: His Ideas and Influence in England and America* (Carbondale: Southern Illinois University Press, 1963), pp. 140–41.
19. Charles Norman quotes Ezra Pound: "'I was in them days [c. 1903–1905] contemplatin a jejune trilogy on Merozia [sic]'" (*Ezra Pound*

"Marozia lived in the eighth or ninth century. She was a woman who was born in very humble conditions. At the age of 16 or 18, she married an unpretentious magistrate—who thanks to the intelligence of his wife became in short time the mayor (?) of the city of Rome. Eight years later he died—and Marozia married the noble X who a short time after the marriage became the duke of Y and attained the highest honors. Eight years later he died and Marozia again married a young magistrate."

[Sophie breaks in] "Yes, who later becomes [the mayor] of Rome and dies eight years later?"

[Pound] "Exactly. You've guessed right. And you think that talented women have no possibility of achieving their goals? That woman was the most powerful person in Rome in that period."

Brzeska objects that a wicked woman can always get her way, and Pound answers, "'I value genius above all. Now that woman certainly had it.'" When she asks what would happen if everyone approved of genius without regard to morality, Gaudier breaks in: "'There! There she is again with her hateful old morality! I tell you that you will never accomplish anything. Your mind turns within a tiny, insignificant sphere.'"

Brzeska disregards Gaudier's provocation and asks Pound if he would like to have a mother, sister, or wife with Marozia's character. Pound replies, "'Oh, I do not take things personally. I admire that woman's genius. We were going to leave, weren't we?'" With this neat dismissal, Pound leaves the Café Royal with the warring couple and walks with them to the underground. Before they part, the two artists agree that Gaudier will carve a bust of Pound.

[New York: Funk & Wagnalls, 1969], p. 356). Marozia (died c. A.D. 945) married in turn Emperor Alberic I, Guido of Tuscany, and Hugh, king of Italy. See Hugh Kenner, *The Pound Era* (Berkeley: University of California Press, 1971), p. 354.

Brzeska's dislike for Pound developed after Gaudier had the singularly bad idea of showing him some of her stories. Pound could not praise them or place them in any magazine with which he was associated—hopes that Gaudier held out to her. Apparently Gaudier also had unrealistic hopes that Pound would support his own work. Brzeska records Gaudier's disappointment at Pound's failure to purchase his alabaster *Stags* before or during the London Group show in March 1914. Gaudier tells her that he is weary of the sessions devoted to sculpting Pound's bust: "'I've had just about enough of him. He comes and stays for hours without speaking. After all, I think that he is superficial, and this idea prevents me from working well on his portrait. —It's not coming along.'" Brzeska comments: "'There's another of your heroes who turns out to be a zero.'"

Nevertheless, the next time Pound is mentioned Gaudier still obviously admires him. When Brzeska and Gaudier attend an exhibition, he leaves her in great excitement to join Pound. Later, when Pound arrives for his final sitting for the *Hieratic Head,* their relations seem quite friendly, and Brzeska is upset that Gaudier invites him to stay for tea. At this meeting Pound announces that he is going to marry Dorothy Shakespear (as he did in April 1914). Brzeska attempts to bait Pound by saying that, although she understands that Dorothy Shakespear is intelligent, he will be able to "excuse" this fault. Pound merely smiles and says that Dorothy is indeed intelligent. Continuing her attack, Brzeska says that she had believed Pound too "advanced" for the institution of marriage. Pound replies:

> "—It doesn't matter. Wife or mistress—it's the same thing. It's just a question of a few procedures for the sake of convenience."

[Brzeska] "Ah, but what if one wishes to separate? Look what terrible chores you'll have to go through."

[Pound] "Why get a divorce? —One lives in mutual tolerance."

[Brzeska] "In that case it's a perfect arrangement—if only one has the nature to agree to it."

[Pound] "Why not? It's simple enough?"

Brzeska wonders if Pound is sincere or if he is only adopting the "business-like" pose of the Englishman.

The last reference to Pound in the diary concerns his review of the London Group show in *The Egoist* of March 16, 1914. Gaudier was depressed over his failure to sell anything at the show, in particular his carved alabaster *Stags.* Pound's review evidently did not improve his mood. Even Pound himself noted that Gaudier resented his allusion in this review to the "Chinese" quality in his work.[20] Brzeska describes the state of Pound and Gaudier's friendship in the spring of 1914 and the effect of the *Egoist* article:

> You have not gone to see Pound for a long time. I am not sure whether it is on my account or yours. He was to write a critique on you in the "Egoiste" . . . he makes almost an apogee |?| [sic] of Epstein—scarcely mentioning you. In two or three very brief sentences he says you are only "in [your] *formative period*" (you who think yourself a master!) and that, even better, "*I would not agree that he is an imitator of Epstein.*" [Brzeska's italics.]

She notes that Gaudier now says that he is through with Pound.

We know that Gaudier was not through with Pound, as their cordial letters written while Gaudier was fighting in France reveal. Nevertheless, Gaudier must have been an-

20. Pound, *Gaudier-Brzeska,* p. 29.

noyed with the *Egoist* review, and Brzeska may have been right to complain about Pound's praise of Epstein over Gaudier. The following excerpt from the review, to which Brzeska refers in her diary, is not particularly favorable to Gaudier:

> It is no use saying that Epstein is Egyptian and that Brzeska is Chinese. Nor would I say that the younger man is a follower of the elder. They approach life in different manners.
>
> Brzeska is in a formative stage, he is abundant and pleasing. His animals have what one can only call a "snuggly," comfortable feeling, that might appeal to a child. A very young child would like them to play with if they were not stone and too heavy.
>
> . . . [Gaudier-]Brzeska is as much concerned with representing certain phases of animal life as is Epstein with presenting some austere permanence; some relation of life and yet outside it.[21]

If Gaudier had exhibited some of his slightly earlier works, such as *Dog* or *Faun,* Pound's criticism might have been adequate. One might then even justify Pound's use of such terms as "snuggly" and "comfortable," which are akin to the term he saves for the worst kind of sculpture, "caressable." But Gaudier had exhibited *Stags,* which cannot be described as "snuggly." The two recumbent animals of this sculpture have as fair a claim to "austere permanence" as anything Epstein had sculpted. Horace Brodzky may be correct in saying that Pound judged Gaudier's works according to how well they fitted his Vorticist theories of abstract form. For example, Pound somehow preferred the awkward geometricizing of Gaudier's *Red Stone Dancer* to the more subtle organic forms of *Stags.* In time Pound might well have

21. Pound, "Exhibition at the Goupil Gallery," *Egoist* 1 (March 16, 1914):109.

appreciated Gaudier's developing "naturalism," just as he came to value Gaudier's work over Epstein's. Pound's *Gaudier-Brzeska* shows that he was open to the ideas Gaudier planned to express in an essay called "The Need for Organic Forms in Sculpture." But the dialogue on the values of abstraction and organic form that they might have had was prevented by Gaudier's death. Pound was then left with the sad task, which was complicated by Brzeska's distrust, of selling Gaudier's remaining sculptures.[22]

Gaudier's aesthetic ideas, which by 1914 were diverging from Pound's, were as mercurial as his life. He wrote to Brzeska concerning his theories, ". . . I'm perpetually modifying them, and I am very glad I do. If I stuck to some fixed idea, I should grow mannered, and so spoil the whole of my development."[23] Gaudier raced through a gamut of styles from Rodinesque modeling of figures in motion to Brancusian carvings. His first great enthusiasm, naturally enough for a Frenchman of his generation, was for Auguste Rodin. He longed to sculpt a standing figure in the style of Rodin's *John the Baptist.* His next great enthusiasm was for carving stone rather than modeling clay, and in this medium he was principally inspired by the experimental work of Jacob Epstein. His other enthusiasms were for primitive and then for abstract art, which soon led him to react against Rodin's example with youthful arrogance. Throughout these phases

22. Pound sold the following sculptures to John Quinn: *Dogs,* marble bas-relief; *Stags,* carving in heavily veined alabaster; and *Birds Erect,* carving in stone. These works are listed in *Paintings and Sculptures: The Renowned Collection of Modern and Ultra-Modern Art Formed by the Late John Quinn* (New York: American Art Association, 1927). The bulk of Gaudier's works came into the hands of H. S. Ede, who has generously preserved them through his bequest of Kettle's Yard to the University of Cambridge. *Stags* is owned by the Art Institute of Chicago.

23. Ede, *Savage Messiah,* p. 102.

his thinking displayed a duality regarding what T. E. Hulme, a close friend of Gaudier's during 1914, called the "geometric" and the "vital."[24] This distinction is basic to Gaudier's late works. But before its effects can be traced, one must note the simpler dichotomy between carving and modeling that concerned Gaudier earlier in his career.

Gaudier wrote that "the sculpture I admire is the work of master craftsmen. Every inch of the surface is won at the point of the chisel—every stroke of the hammer is a physical and mental effort."[25] His first significant sculpture was a direct response to the challenge of carving. Ezra Pound tells the story of this first carving. When Gaudier first met Epstein, the older artist said,

> mustering the thunders of god and the scowlings of Assyrian sculpture into his tone and eyebrows, "ummhh! Do . . . you cut . . . direct . . . in stone?"
>
> "Most certainly!" said Gaudier, who had never yet done anything of the sort.
>
> "That's right," said Epstein; "I will come around to your place on Sunday."[26]

Lest his bluff be called, Gaudier worked night and day to prepare for the visit and produced, among other works, *Head of a Boy.* This rather too rounded head with its lumpish nose and inexpressive mouth is nevertheless a fine piece of apprentice work. About twelve inches high, it is carved in

24. T. E. Hulme, who was deeply influenced by the German critic Wilhelm Worringer, made this distinction in his lecture "Modern Art," which was published posthumously by Herbert Read in *Speculations: Essays on Humanism and the Philosophy of Art* (London: Kegan Paul, 1936). Read has since developed the "geometric-vital" principle in numerous works on modern art.

25. Henri Gaudier-Brzeska, "Allied Artists' Association Ltd.," *Egoist* 1 (June 15, 1914):227.

26. Pound, *Gaudier-Brzeska,* p. 76.

sandstone, with the marks of the claw chisel clearly proclaiming it a carved work.

Despite his conviction of the superiority of carved works, he produced few such works in 1911 and 1912. Not only had he much to learn about carving, but he was so impoverished that he was not able to buy suitable stones. Some of the stones he did use were snatched from stonemason yards. (The scene in Ken Russell's film *Savage Messiah* in which Gaudier makes a night raid on a cemetery and carts off a marble grave marker is not altogether an exaggeration.) While still under Rodin's spell in 1912, he produced a series of acute character studies in a freely modeled style that also shows the influence of Epstein's portrait heads. The finest works of 1912 are not sculptures, however, but drawings. These drawings are characterized by a calligraphic line that Gaudier described as being "in the Chinese manner." His drawing of a wolf (Fig. 3), which was inspired by Pound's "Piere Vidal Old," conveys the animal's nervous strength through the tense lines of its legs and paws. Although Gaudier's drawings demonstrate a mastery of line, he considered line "illusory": "Line is a bar, a limit, an infraction of liberty, a slavery—while mass is free, and can be multiplied infinitely, treated in a thousand ways."[27] Gaudier's later drawings emphasize the three-dimensional planes of a figure, as in the charcoal nudes at the Victoria and Albert Museum in London, and in the drawings of Ezra Pound, which were made by a stick daubed in ink.

Gaudier considered sculpture superior to both drawing and painting. An anti-Impressionist, he felt that color was less basic than form. He wrote that "sculpture is the art of expressing the reality of ideas in the most palpable

27. Ede, *Savage Messiah,* p. 48.

3. Henri Gaudier-Brzeska, *Wolf.* Victoria and Albert Museum, London.

form. . . . civilizations begin with sculpture and end with it. Painting, music, letters, are all later refinements."[28] He did, however, produce a fine portrait, in vivid, hot colors, of Sophie Brzeska (Fig. 4). He explains the technique of this work in a letter to a patron as the "optic mixing of the colors—putting them in pure pigments side by side so as to give the resulting tone."[29] This painting integrates the sensitive line that is characteristic of his drawings (as in the portrait's profiled face) with an almost expressionistic background.

While he drew and painted, Gaudier still longed to sculpt. He wrote to a friend in July 1912 about his dream of a one-man show of his sculpture: "I have for years been studying character almost to the exclusion of rhythm and composition and confined myself to the drawing of people's faces. . . . the unsettled life I have been leading up to now has only allowed me to work [on sculpture] a little here and there."[30]

During his last two frantic years in England, Gaudier concentrated on his sculpting, even quitting his job as a translator and clerk sometime in 1913 to gain time to establish himself as a sculptor. Much of his sculpture produced in 1913 does not demonstrate the subordination of character to sculptural form that he was trying to achieve. His portrait bust *Horace Brodzky,* for example, has an almost baroque flair in its heroic characterization of the painter. In comparison with Epstein's work, which is a clear influence on the *Brodzky,* its characterization has little depth. Gaudier does have some success, however, in defining the planes of the face and in the undulating treatment of the

28. Ibid., p. 22.
29. Gaudier to Haldane Macfall, February 26, 1912. By courtesy of the Victoria and Albert Museum Library, London.
30. Ibid.

4. Henri Gaudier-Brzeska, *Sophie Brzeska*. The Tate Gallery, London.

82

sitter's chest. His portrait head of the painter Alfred Wolmark is equally flamboyant in its treatment of Wolmark's
hooked nose and streaming hair. A touch of humor and
irony save both works from bombast.

Gaudier also molded portrait heads of Middleton Murry,
whose journal *Rhythm* had published some of Gaudier's
drawings, and of Brzeska. These heads have not survived.
Gaudier had the terrifying habit (as Horace Brodzky considered it) of treating his works as if they were animate and
attacking them amorously or aggressively. The head of
Brzeska, which even she thought successful, was destroyed
during one of their furious arguments. After she broke up
Gaudier's intense friendship with Murry, the editor was
ritually "killed" by having his clay likeness smashed.
Brodzky recalls that after a discussion of Murry's character,
"we dashed into the studio and Henri quickly found and
fished out the unlucky head, which happened to be hardened
clay. Sophie shrieked. The unoffending head was placed
against the wall, a little grayish target. . . . Then, 'Beast!'
shrieked Sophie as we each armed ourselves with a brick."[31]
By smashing the head, Henri had proved his loyalty to
Sophie.

The masterpiece of Gaudier's molded sculptures finally
succeeds in subordinating character to rhythm. *The Dancer*
of 1913 (Fig. 5) presents an impersonal face in a statue that
from any viewpoint displays tense, powerful lines. Stanley
Casson describes the spiral movement of the dancer's turn:
"There is no torsion and no confusion of curves . . . movement is detected rather than seen, and detected at a moment
when it is neither static nor in motion, when it is potential
and yet not stopped. . . . Rodin's definition of movement as

31. Brodzky, *Henri Gaudier-Brzeska,* pp. 45–46.

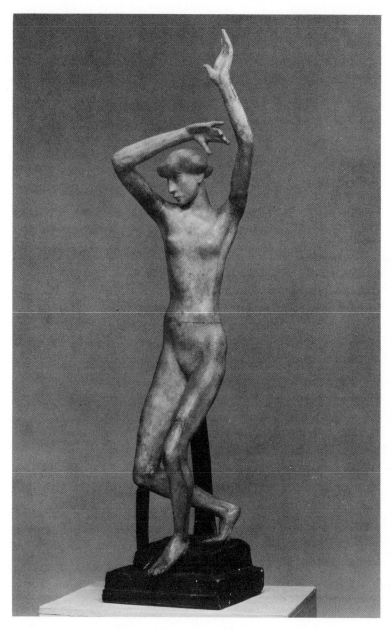

5. Henri Gaudier-Brzeska, *The Dancer*. The Tate Gallery, London.

'transition' is here carried out more clearly than he could ever have wished."[32] This sense of movement is accentuated by the elongation of the dancer's limbs and torso and by the simple device of having one of the figure's feet step down off the plinth.

Gaudier compresses a similar grace of line into a carved figure of 1913, *Maternité*. Although it does not have the exciting lines and expression of movement of *The Dancer,* the carving achieves greater compactness and solidity. In these two works one sees a transition between styles that is something more than the difference in qualities expected when one moves from a molded to a carved work. Gaudier wrote in 1912 that he was a disciple of Bergson and believed that "life . . . is simply intuition of the passing moment, and time, which flows continually, eternally, makes itself known by change." This romantic conviction underlies *The Dancer* and leads to his theory that "movement is the translation of life, and if art depicts life, movement should come into art, since we are only aware of life because it moves."[33] This aesthetic of movement left him as he tried to produce more compact, static masses. His new artistic goal is evident in a severely perpendicular work he carved from Derby stone in the spring of 1913, *La Chanteuse triste*. It expresses a moment of complete stillness as the singer crosses her arms behind her back in a pose of intense self-absorption. This work, in which Ezra Pound detected an archaic Greek influence, is not one of Gaudier's strongest carvings. The torso's middle is rather shapeless and the drapery around the bottom of the figure imparts little interest to the design. But the work does show the mastery of line that never deserted

32. Stanley Casson, *Some Modern Sculptors* (Oxford: Oxford University Press, 1928), pp. 97–98.
33. Ede, *Savage Messiah,* p. 98.

Gaudier in the figure's silhouette, which a French critic has called a *fillet de fume*.[34]

In 1914 Gaudier produced a series of fine sculptures. Although the geometric-vital distinction is central to them all, at least three styles may be distinguished in these works. There are "Vorticist" works, such as *Bird Swallowing a Fish* and *Toy*; primitivistic works, such as *Red Stone Dancer, Seated Woman,* and *Hieratic Head of Ezra Pound*; and vitalistic works, such as *Stags* and *Birds Erect*. Rough as they are, these overlapping categories indicate the remarkably varied achievements of Gaudier's brief career.

The term *Vorticist* is particularly difficult to apply to Gaudier, even though the only important critical studies of Gaudier, Pound's *Gaudier-Brzeska* (1915) and Richard Cork's *Vorticism* (1976), have placed him squarely within that movement. Despite Gaudier's appearance in the Vorticist journal *Blast,* he does not seem to have been any more loyal to Vorticism than he was to Roger Fry's Omega Workshops. Although the Vorticists considered Fry a bitter enemy, Gaudier continued to receive commissions from the Omega until his last days in England. Gaudier possessed an innocent opportunism that allowed him to align himself with both of the rival groups without irritating either. After his death, while Pound claimed him as one of the *Blast* group, Roger Fry said that Gaudier intended to abandon Vorticism and "return to organic forms."[35]

What did it mean to be a Vorticist sculptor? The movement's technical innovations were inspired by Cubism, and it

34. Jérôme Peignot, "Henri Gaudier-Brzeska," *Connaissance des Arts,* May 1965, p. 71.

35. Roger Fry, "Gaudier-Brzeska," *Burlington Magazine* 29 (August 1916):210. Wyndham Lewis himself considered Gaudier "a good man on the soft side . . . not 'one of us'" (*Rude Assignment* [London: Hutchinson, 1950], p. 128).

drew its awareness of modern industrial life and machine forms in part from Futurism. The movement's truly distinctive feature was its use of total abstraction. Wyndham Lewis wrote in 1956 that Vorticism sought "to build up a visual language as abstract as music."[36] The vocabulary of this visual language was to come from synthetic rather than natural forms. The Vorticists admired the power, the hardness, and even the brutality of machine forms. If a Vorticist were to use natural forms, Lewis explained, "a shape represented by a fish remained a form independent of that animal, and could be made use of in a universe in which there was no fish."[37] But the preferred course, as in Lewis's *Plan of War* and *Red Duet,* was to avoid if possible all reference to natural forms.

The difficulty of interpreting Gaudier's work as Vorticist is seen in Richard Cork's reference to *Bird Swallowing a Fish* (Fig. 6) as a "cold and brutal Vorticist image": "Completely ignoring *Blast* no. 1's injunction to feed off industrial subject matter, he has nevertheless succeeded in producing a mechanistic image full of the cold dehumanization which characterizes the movement as a whole."[38] Yet Gaudier presents the bird's swallowing a fish as the everyday natural event that it is; the "merciless swiftness" and "sinister malignance" that Cork discovers could arise only if one sentimentalized the fate of the fish, which Gaudier does not do.[39] There is great calm in the heavy mass of the bird, which is saved from

36. Lewis, *Wyndham Lewis on Art,* ed. Walter Michel and C. J. Fox (New York: Funk & Wagnalls, 1969), p. 452.
37. Ibid.
38. Richard Cork, *Vorticism and Its Allies* (London: Hayward Gallery, Arts Council of Great Britain, 27 March–2 June 1974), p. 70.
39. Richard Cork, *Vorticism and Abstract Art in the First Machine Age,* 2 vols. (Berkeley and Los Angeles: University of California Press, 1976), 2:438.

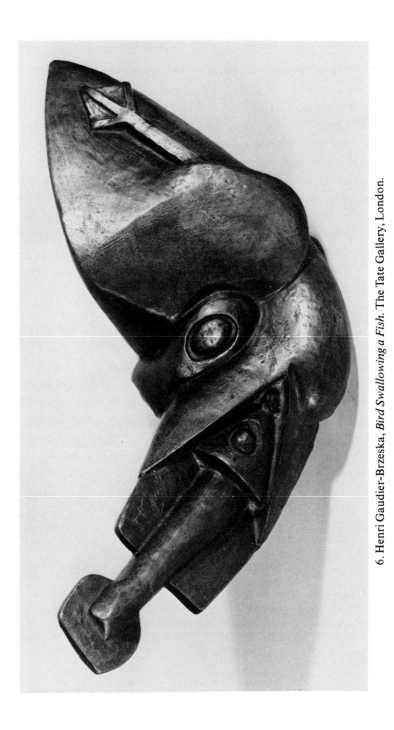

6. Henri Gaudier-Brzeska, *Bird Swallowing a Fish*. The Tate Gallery, London.

stolidity through the superb tension of the work's inverted arch.

Gaudier nevertheless absorbed enough Vorticism to understand that the use of abstraction was the movement's most significant innovation. He wrote in *Blast,* no. 2, "I shall present my emotions by the ARRANGEMENT OF MY SURFACES, THE PLANES AND LINES BY WHICH THEY ARE DEFINED." [40] *In Bird Swallowing a Fish* he emphasizes the geometric construction of both bird and fish: the square, rectangular, and cone shapes of the fish, and the arched back and spherical eyes of the bird. As in Lewis's formulation, the forms of bird and fish seem independent of the creatures that exist in the natural world.

Gaudier never produced a work so distinctively Vorticist as Epstein's *Rock Drill,* and Epstein himself never supported the movement beyond contributing some drawings to *Blast,* no. 1. The closest Gaudier came to a truly Vorticist work was his brass sculpture *Toy* (Fig. 7). He cut this small sculpture out of solid brass so that the forms would "gain in sharpness and rigidity." [41] The use of triangular forms as well as the suggestion of a manlike figure—the new Machine Age man of the Futurists and Vorticists—is characteristic of Wyndham Lewis's work as well. *Toy's* geometric qualities also recall Gaudier's relationship with T. E. Hulme; indeed, he made the six-inch-high figure for Hulme as a kind of talisman. (Gaudier also cut knuckle-dusters of solid brass for both Hulme and Wyndham Lewis, who were notoriously aggressive men.) Gaudier revealed Hulme's influence when he wrote to a conservative friend early in 1915 that naturalism is a "hollow accomplishment: the artificial is full of metaphysical meaning, which is all important." [42] A passage from

40. Pound, *Gaudier-Brzeska,* p. 28.
41. Gaudier, "Allied Artists' Association," p. 228.
42. Ede, *Savage Messiah,* p. 151.

7. Henri Gaudier-Brzeska, *Toy (Ornament)*. The Tate Gallery, London.

T. E. Hulme's famous lecture "Modern Art," which was delivered in February 1914 to an audience of incipient Vorticists, shows what Gaudier means by the "metaphysical meaning" of the artificial. Hulme said that "vital art" expresses a "feeling of increased vitality" that results from a "happy pantheistic relation between man and the outside world." Like the Vorticists, Hulme felt that modern man must abandon a naive, romantic faith in nature. The really modern artist desires "to create a certain abstract geometrical shape, which, being durable and permanent shall be a refuge from the flux and impermanence of outside nature. . . . In the reproduction of natural objects there is an attempt to purify them of their characteristically living qualities. . . . This leads to rigid lines and dead crystalline forms."[43]

Hulme's requirements for modern art can all be found in *Toy*. Yet Gaudier did not adhere to them for long. Epstein was right when he called Gaudier a follower of styles.[44] Even in the brilliant use of pierced forms in *Toy*—the triangles at each extremity are cut clear through to the other side—he was probably following Alexander Archipenko's lead. When the various styles are used so confidently, this imitative quality is no fault in a young sculptor. *Toy*, however, displays a quality that is individual and consistent. The design of his most geometric work not only suggests a man (however machine-like) but also, if it is turned on its side, a fish.[45] His concern for organic form persists even in the work most nearly related to Vorticist theories.

43. T. E. Hulme, "Modern Art," pp. 86–87.
44. Epstein, *Let There Be Sculpture,* p. 36. Epstein says that "far from innovating, Gaudier always followed. He followed quickly, overnight."
45. Gaudier also referred to *Toy* as "Ornament, torpille!" See the list of Gaudier's works in the 1930 edition of *Savage Messiah* (London: William Heinemann). A *torpille* is a torpedo fish.

The importance of primitivism to Gaudier is indicated by the name his friends half-mockingly gave him and in which he delighted: "Savage Messiah." This primitivism is particularly clear in one of his best-known works, *Red Stone Dancer* (Fig. 8). Ezra Pound singled this work out for special praise and, while acknowledging that it was inspired by African art, described it as if it were a thesis demonstration of Vorticist ideas on pure form:

> We have the triangle and circle asserted, *labeled* almost, upon the face and right breast. Into these so-called "abstractions" life flows, the circle moves and elongates into the oval, it increases and takes volume in the sphere or hemisphere of the breast. . . . These two developed motifs work as themes in a fugue. We have the whole series of spherical triangles, as in the arm over the head. . . . The whole form-series ends, passes into stasis with the circular base or platform.[46]

Although this is a fine description of Gaudier's use of geometric, "musical" form, the weakness of the sculpture's design is suggested in Pound's use of the italicized word *labeled* to indicate the way the circle and triangle are used. The triangle of the face and the circle of the breast seem two-dimensional—applied like a label—rather than sculptural. Moreover, the figure's squatness, which reveals the African influence, is not integrated with the very Western expression of movement in the sculpture. Brzeska records that Gaudier often criticized his own works for not being "simple enough," and we might say the same of *Red Stone Dancer*. Pound does describe the work's strength, however, when he enthusiastically praises the triangular forms that culminate "in the great sweep of the back of the shoulders, as fine as any surface in all sculpture."[47]

46. Pound, *Gaudier-Brzeska,* pp. 137–38.
47. Ibid., p. 138.

8. Henri Gaudier-Brzeska, *Red Stone Dancer*. The Tate Gallery, London.

Two other works in which primitive influence is strong are important. In *Hieratic Head of Ezra Pound* Gaudier imparts to the three-foot-high marble block (the largest piece of stone he ever had to work with and a gift from Pound himself) the monumentality of an Easter Island megalith.[48] The idea of shaping his subject in a form that suggests a phallus, which Pound's theories of the link between sex and creative genius made entirely appropriate, is detectable, as in Rodin's *Balzac,* from a side view. Pound is commonly described as the seminal figure of modern poetry, a notion this sculpture takes literally. (Pound said that Lewis's first portrait of him—1919, now lost—was also phallic. Under the pseudonym of B. H. Dias, Pound wrote that Lewis's portrait "rises with the dignity of a classic *stele* to the god of gardens.")[49] Gaudier's other important primitivistic work is *Seated Woman,* which Gaudier himself referred to as "Sleeping Woman." The woman's arms are crossed with her hand behind her head in the conventional pose of the sleeper. One arm juts out and forms a magnificent triangular volume. The striations of the carved marble beautifully accentuate the sinuous curve of the back. Nowhere is Gaudier's sensitivity to the material with which he is working better seen than in this sculpture. The white stone perfectly suits the form of the sleeper, as does the masklike, utterly quiet face (which reveals the primitive influence as transformed by Modigliani).

The vitalistic phase of Gaudier's career produced two of his greatest works, *Stags* and *Birds Erect.* Although these works are perhaps no finer than *Dancer, Mlle B.,* or *Seated*

48. See Cork, *Vorticism and Abstract Art,* 1:182 on the Easter Island influence.

49. B. H. Dias [Ezra Pound], "Art Notes," *New Age* 26 (December 11, 1919):96.

Woman, they are more original and more suggestive of the way he was developing at the time of his death. They may be called vitalistic in the sense that Henry Moore (an admirer of Gaudier who once owned *Bird Swallowing a Fish*) uses the term: "a vitality from inside it, so that you have a sense that the form is pressing from inside trying to burst or trying to give off the strength from inside itself, rather than having something which is just shaped from outside and stopped."[50] Gaudier's vitalism represented a total and quite sudden reaction to T. E. Hulme's antinaturalism and was directly influenced by Constantin Brancusi, whom Gaudier met in London in 1913. He also shared with Brancusi a respect for Henri Bergson's concept of the *élan vital.* Gaudier's new ambition to capture the vital form inherent in the stone he was carving was of course related to the traditional sculptural idea that the carver releases a form that is implicit in the stone. Earlier Gaudier had linked carving to the creation of geometric works and molding to naturalistic works. The will of the carver was to stamp his design on the resisting material. He had this concept in mind when he wrote in his "Vortex" for *Blast,* no. 1, "Will and consciousness are our VORTEX."[51] In his vitalistic phase, he believed that the sculptor releases rather than imposes form.

In *Stags* (Fig. 9), a sculpture in pink-veined alabaster, as in *Seated Woman,* the striation of the stone is used to beautiful effect. Measuring about three feet by two, it is the most compact of Gaudier's sculptures. The stags are asleep,

50. Philip James, ed., *Henry Moore on Sculpture* (New York: Viking Press, 1966), p. 60. Moore has said of Gaudier, "[Gaudier] a donné la certitude qu'en cherchant à créer selon d'autres voies que celles de la sculpture traditionelle, on pouvait atteindre à la beauté, puisque Gaudier l'avait réussi" (René Varin, *Henri Gaudier, sculpteur orléanais, 1891–1915* [Orléans: Musée des Beaux-Arts d'Orléans, March–April 1956], pp. 7–8).
51. Pound, *Gaudier-Brzeska,* p. 24.

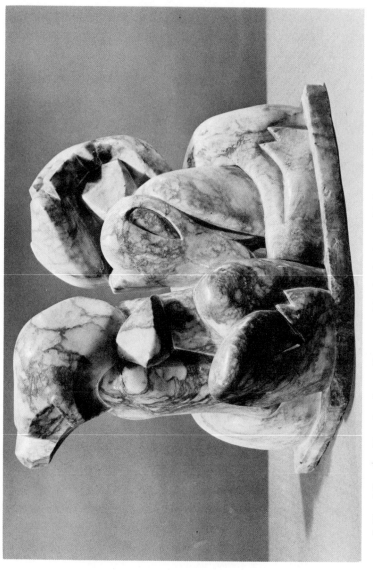

9. Henri Gaudier-Brzeska, *Stags*. Courtesy of the Art Institute of Chicago. Gift of Samuel Lustgarten.

their legs drawn up to their bodies, and the head of one stag is pressed against the side of the other. The work expresses an un-Vorticist tenderness and quiet. The animal forms are not really naturalistic, however; these sleeping stags are as heavily stylized as Gaudier's sleeping woman. From certain viewpoints, their figures suggest rock and plant forms as well as the phallic shape that was rarely absent from his late works. The shapes that appear where one would expect to see the stags' antlers are treated most freely, suggesting organic forms as different as a rock formation and the calyx of a flower. Seen from the rear, the flower formation stands out. Viewed directly from above, the concave mass of the antlers is seen to be a vortex.

Birds Erect (Fig. 10) is the most suggestive of all Gaudier's works. This sculpture is related to the last work he carved, a garden urn commissioned through the Omega Workshops, which, depending on the perspective, presents the form of either a ram or a girl. *Birds Erect* shows a mother bird with a swelling breast perched above her two fledglings, who turn and stretch their necks toward her with open beaks. Although the design is even more formalized than that of *Stags,* the shapes of the birds are clearly recognizable. The forms are also inspired, as an early drawing for the sculpture shows, by the thrusting forms of a cactus plant that Gaudier owned. This relating of natural forms was a technique that came readily to him. Like Henry Moore, he was an enthusiastic naturalist. He once wrote that he admired a certain friend because, like himself, "he has studied and adored ferns, the reproduction of plants, sea-stars, the collection and life of shell-fish, flowers, insects."[52] A third major form in *Birds Erect,* as indicated by the title, is the phallus, which

52. Ede, *Savage Messiah,* p. 124.

10. Henri Gaudier-Brzeska, *Birds Erect.* Limestone, 26⅝″ × 10¼″ × 12⅜″. Collection, The Museum of Modern Art, New York. Gift of Mrs. W. Murray Crane.

is more explicitly represented than it is in the head of Ezra Pound. These three major analogized forms are not the only ones the sculpture contains. For example, from one angle the work resembles the flank of an animal, and from another it suggests mountain peaks. This work is Gaudier's most original sculpture and indicates that, his apprenticeship over, he was ready to define and develop his own style.

Gaudier's personal style, as expressed in *Birds Erect,* must be distinguished from the experimental styles of an epoch bursting with new movements and theories. When Ezra Pound claimed that Gaudier's best work was Vorticist and Horace Brodzky that Gaudier's "real work" was "naturalistic," they were merely applying current labels to his work without describing its individuality.[53] Writing soon after his death and as personal friends, they naturally lacked perspective. Yet even during Gaudier's lifetime there was a constant factor in the controversies surrounding such movements as Post-Impressionism, Cubism, Futurism, and Vorticism which could have clarified Gaudier's art. The dualism in his thinking moved from "carving and molding" through "geometric and vital" to the polarity that underlies most aesthetic theories, "nature and art," and finally to a synthesis that escaped these theoretic limits.

Pre–World War I London debated the age-old question of nature versus art as energetically as the ages of Hogarth and Fielding, Wordsworth and Turner, Wilde and Whistler. Indeed, the twentieth-century debate took its theme directly from the Wilde-Whistler controversies of the 1880s. J. A. M. Whistler's lecture "Ten O'Clock" informed the philistine public that "Nature is usually wrong" as a model for art, and

53. Brodzky, *Henri Gaudier-Brzeska,* pp. 94, 97.

Oscar Wilde's "Decay of Lying" laid down the "doctrine" that "all bad art comes from returning to Life and Nature."[54] The Vorticists, taking the antinature propaganda of the 1880s quite literally, proposed to banish nature from their canvases and not simply to rearrange its elements, more or less boldly, as Whistler did. Lewis said that the artist should absorb nature's power rather than imitate its surfaces in order to invent totally synthetic forms. In *Blast,* Lewis proclaimed that modern art must keep pace with an industrial society that "has reared up steel trees where the green ones were lacking; has exploded in useful growths, and found wilder intricacies than those of Nature."[55]

In such works as *Red Duet* and the drawings of his 1914 notebooks (which resemble computer circuits), Lewis avoided any reference to external nature. But he discovered that his austere techniques led to arid, dehumanized works. Years later Lewis explained that in 1914 the Vorticist aesthetic was tempting him "to fly away from the world of men, of pigs, of chickens and alligators, and to go to live in the unwatered moon, only a moon sawed up into square blocks, in the most alarming way. What an escape I had!"[56] Lewis escaped back to nature, and to the dismay of his more radical supporters (including Ezra Pound), his postwar pictures were chiefly representational. Yet this sudden turn to the side of nature in the nature/art debate was not totally unexpected, since even Lewis the Vorticist admitted that all art contained an "unavoidable representative element."[57] He

54. J. A. M. Whistler, "Ten O'Clock," in Denys Sutton, *James McNeill Whistler* (London: Phaidon Press, 1966), p. 53; Oscar Wilde, "The Decay of Lying," in *Aesthetes and Decadents of the 1890's,* ed. Karl Beckson (New York: Random House, 1966), p. 193.
55. *Wyndham Lewis on Art,* p. 29.
56. Wyndham Lewis, *The Demon of Progress in the Arts* (London: Methuen, 1954), p. 3.
57. *Wyndham Lewis on Art,* p. 73.

reasoned that even a collection of geometric squares, cubes, or arcs inevitably evoked pebbles or leaves or ocean waves from nature's storehouse of forms.

T. E. Hulme insisted that abstract forms necessarily depend on the material universe well before Lewis did. Although Hulme is often considered a champion of abstract art, his "Modern Art" articles for *New Age* were extremely conservative and unfriendly to most experimental art, aside from that of his friend Jacob Epstein. In his most radical work, a lecture called "Modern Art," Hulme said that abstraction was necessary to save one from "the flux and impermanence of outside nature." Yet he also said that the desire for abstraction "cannot be satisfied with the reproduction of merely inorganic forms."[58] This statement shows why Hulme did not rally to the Vorticists, whose works took Hulme's own ideas to radical conclusions that he distrusted.

In his *New Age* articles, Hulme's conservatism is still more pronounced. His essay "Neo-Realism" states: "There must be just as much contact with nature in an abstract art as in a realist one. . . . But in as far as the artist is creative, he is not bound down by the accidental relations of the elements actually found in nature."[59] This opinion does not advance beyond Whistler's theories, and its staleness prepares us for Hulme's weak comment on Gaudier's exhibition at the London Group show: "I admire the ability of Mr. Gaudier-Brzeska's sculpture; the tendencies it displays are sound though the abstractions used do not seem to be always thoroughly thought out."[60] This cursory remark is the whole of Hulme's criticism of Gaudier's work. Ironically, Gaudier's achievement lay precisely in thinking through the issues that

58. Hulme, "Modern Art," p. 106.
59. Hulme, *Further Speculations by T. E. Hulme,* ed. Sam Hynes (Minneapolis: University of Minnesota Press), p. 128.
60. Hulme, "The London Group," in *Further Speculations,* p. 132.

puzzled both Hulme and Lewis with a coherence that Lewis would match only in his postwar art criticism. Gaudier found a way between Lewis's Vorticist extremism and Hulme's timid traditionalism.

Gaudier's only explanation of his mature aesthetic, and a curtly expressed one at that, is the "Vortex" he wrote for *Blast,* no. 1. This two-page "history of form value," as he called it, is a brilliant foreword, or vor-text, to modern sculpture and left its mark on Henry Moore's prose for *Unit 1* in 1934. Gaudier connects a preference for cylindrical, vertical, or horizontal sculptural forms with the values of the civilization that favored them. He holds that the modern sculptor is self-conscious enough to use all possible form combinations for their own sakes. He does not have to depend on the vertical, as the Egyptian sculptor did, to inspire religious awe, or on squat, massive forms, as in the Assyrian "man-headed bulls in horizontal flight-walk," to communicate a civilization's power. Nevertheless, Gaudier himself shows a clear preference for the forms used by primitive cultures. His comment on the cultures of Africa and Oceania reflect back on his own art: "Their expenditure of energy was wide, for they began to till the land and practice crafts rationally, and they fell into contemplation before their sex: the site of their great energy: THEIR CONVEX MATURITY."[61]

Hulme claimed that primitive art expressed a terror of external nature. Gaudier, on the contrary, praised the sexual energy that allowed primitive races to master nature, an achievement that they expressed artistically through "THEIR CONVEX MATURITY." This obscure term, printed in the bold-face type that *Blast* used to emphasize its most explosive

61. Pound, *Gaudier-Brzeska,* p. 23.

ideas, is clarified a bit when Gaudier writes that "PLASTIC SOUL IS INTENSITY OF LIFE BURSTING THE PLANE." Impelled by this energy, the primitive sculptor "pulled the sphere length-ways and made the cylinder, this is the VORTEX OF FECUN-DITY." According to Gaudier, "VORTEX IS ENERGY!"[62] The primitive sculptor found a form expressive of this power, basically sexual in character, which energizes all of nature.

Thus Gaudier's "Vorticism" was really a form of vitalism. Indeed, Jack Burnham links Gaudier with Brancusi as one of the "pioneer vitalists."[63] A term more relevant to the period than *vitalism,* however, would be *organicism,* since theories of organic form dominated the arts in England from at least the nineteenth century on. Roger Fry wrote in 1916 that even in Gaudier's Vorticist experiments, "the general princi-ples of organic form are still adhered to, the plasticity is rounded with a peculiar bluntness and yet sweetness of form, but it remains sensitive and full of life."[64]

Gaudier was planning to announce his decision to use organic form in the never published third issue of *Blast.* According to Pound, who realized that this decision would challenge Vorticist ways of thinking, Gaudier's essay "The Need of Organic Forms in Sculpture" would have said that inorganic forms were more suitable for painting than for sculpture "because in painting one can have a much greater complexity, a much greater number of form units than in sculpture." Without explaining why sculpture demands a simpler overall form, Pound continues that a second reason that Gaudier wished to use organic forms was that "machin-ery itself has used up so many of the fine combinations of

62. Ibid., pp. 22–23.
63. Jack Burnham, *Beyond Modern Sculpture* (New York: George Braziller, 1967), p. 80.
64. Fry, "Gaudier-Brzeska," p. 210.

three dimensional inorganic forms that there is very little use in experimenting with them in sculpture."[65] Perhaps Epstein sensed this second point when he mounted his *Rock Drill* sculpture on a real pneumatic drill, as if to acknowledge the impressive forms that modern machines could achieve.

Pound says that his summary of Gaudier's new position is "very rough and clumsy." Yet his account shows clearly that Gaudier's move toward conscious organicism was based on his perception of the difference between painted and sculpted forms and in part reflects his conviction that sculpture is a more primitive art than painting. Wyndham Lewis also considered sculpture more inherently organic or vitalistic than painting because it used three dimensions. To Lewis, who made the failed artist in his 1918 novel *Tarr* a sculptor, sculptural art seemed to have an inherent weakness. Even in 1950, Lewis could write that the "third dimension is dangerous for the European artist: there lies in wait for him the naturalistic canon of tradition as nowhere else. The second dimension is, by reason of its limitation, less prone to perpetrate this ancestral vitalist mistake."[66] Gaudier in effect accepted Lewis's reasoning about the inherent vitalism of three-dimensional art. But he saw, with an insight greater than Lewis's, that sculpture could express a vitalist spirit without using merely imitative or naturalistic forms.

Vorticism's ultimate value for Gaudier was to teach him how to "abstract" form from the chaotic variety of nature's forms. While drawing these shapes from organic nature, he synthesized them into designs whose rhythms are satisfying in themselves. Jack Burnham writes that Gaudier wished to

65. Pound, *Gaudier-Brzeska*, p. 26.
66. Lewis, *The Letters of Wyndham Lewis*, ed. W. K. Rose (Norfolk, Conn.: New Directions, 1963), p. 529.

"carve nature-originated forms without betraying their source."[67] But it is more likely that Gaudier wished the viewer to recognize the sources, though not at the risk of spoiling the design, in order to appreciate the metamorphosis created by the sculpture. In his postwar criticism Wyndham Lewis held that the tension between a work's formal design and its representational form enriched the work. The artist achieves this effect, Lewis wrote in a memorable phrase, by "burying Euclid deep in the living flesh."[68]

Birds Erect achieves this richness of design. The convex swelling of the mother bird's breast and the forms of the smaller birds, surging up at a tangent to her breast, present a design more complex and energetic than that of *Bird Swallowing a Fish*. *Birds Erect* is also more coherent stylistically than *Stags*, since it avoids the latter's somewhat jarring contrast of representational and abstracted forms. The phallic reference of *Birds Erect* recalls Gaudier's statement that sex is the "site" of primitive energy. The energy expressed by the phallic, animal, and plant forms of the work is the sexual power of growth and development. Gaudier did not merely rearrange nature's elements, as Hulme prescribed, or cut himself off from its influence, as the Vorticists required. Instead he evoked the organic force that courses through all objects in nature. In this use of the organic, Gaudier resembled Jean Arp, whose playful temperament and aesthetic adventurousness were much like Gaudier's.

During their last days together in the spring of 1914, Sophie and Henri often visited Richmond Park to see the flowers and deer. H. S. Ede writes that on one such visit Henri "was so entranced with the beauty of nature that he

67. Burnham, *Beyond Modern Sculpture,* p. 83.
68. *Wyndham Lewis on Art,* p. 330.

said he would probably return to a naturalistic style in his work."[69] Sophie's diary reveals, however, that Henri had more to say. She used his declaration to strengthen her own argument that "abstract" art spoiled his true talent. She scorned *Birds Erect* as "three corkscrews in stone" (at least noticing its spiral or vorticist pattern). He was annoyed and remarked, as he had so constantly in the past, that she understood nothing about art. A tear in the manuscript deletes some of his words, but it is clear that he dismissed her conception of beauty. He asked her where one finds the beauty of nature and said that he found it in the geometric surfaces that he perceived within nature. He was no longer distracted by such distinctions as Brzeska raised between art and nature, or by Hulme's more sophisticated dichotomy of geometric and vital. He had found his own synthesis of geometric and natural forms. Gaudier's spirit was as experimental and original as Lewis's or Pound's, but his mind was more flexible and the range of his achievements before 1915 greater. Lewis and Pound never forgot him as a personality, and their appreciation of his artistic principles grew with the years.

69. Ede, *Savage Messiah,* p. 154.

4

Nature and Art
in the Vortex

To copy nature is a spineless activity. . . . But to imitate nature
involves the verb: we then ourselves become nature, and so
invent an object which is an extension of the process.
—William Carlos Williams

In 1956 Pound wrote to Lewis: "Have always held re/
vortex, dominant cell in somatic devilupment, convergence
in atom structure, etc." Pound reminisced about Vorticism in
numerous letters to Lewis (whom he called the "Vort") in the
1950s. When the two men discussed plans for a permanent
Vorticism room at London's Tate Gallery, Pound defined
Vorticist art in his typically abrupt manner: "works showing
understanding of basic forms, both in natr/ and ON the
kanVASS."[1] This emphasis on form "in natr/" shows how far
Pound had moved from the antinature propaganda of the
1914 Vorticists. The same emphasis governs his claim that
the term "*Blast*" was "connected in the arcane recesses of
Mr. Lewis's mind with blastoderms and sources of life."[2]
Pound's new understanding of Vorticism's goals indicates an
important line of his aesthetic "devilupment" as well as the
development of Wyndham Lewis as a painter. Both moved

1. Ezra Pound to Wyndham Lewis, December 7, 1956, and n.d. (sent
from St. Elizabeths Hospital in the 1950s), Olin Library, Cornell University.
2. Ezra Pound, *If This Be Treason* (Siena: printed for Olga Rudge by
Tipografia Nuova, 1948), p. 29.

from an ambiguous repudiation of natural forms to a clear affirmation of their crucial importance for the artist.

In an account of the *Blast* period, Ezra Pound complained (pointedly, since he was writing in T. S. Eliot's *Criterion*) that the public did not see that Lewis equaled or surpassed Eliot as a critic.[3] Lewis's greatest contribution to critical thought was his reanimation of the nature versus art debate, which had cooled down since the days of Oscar Wilde and James McNeill Whistler. Lewis poses the issue in the block-shaped letters of a manifesto he wrote for *Blast*:

> BLESS the HAIRDRESSER
> He attacks Mother Nature for a small fee. . . .
> He trims aimless and retrograde growths
> into CLEAN ARCHED SHAPES and
> ANGULAR PLOTS.[4]

This high-spirited passage recalls Max Beerbohm's praise of cosmetics in *The Yellow Book,* as other passages recall Wilde's famous contention that nature imitates art rather than the reverse. The play Lewis published in the 1914 *Blast, Enemy of the Stars,* might almost illustrate Wilde's dictum "Nature hates Mind."[5] Lewis's Beckett-like monodrama portrays the destruction of the artist's mind through his own physical, emotional nature as well as through the cosmic power symbolized by the stars.

Lewis, however, explicitly rejects Wilde and "THE BRITANNIC AESTHETE." For despite Wilde's attacks on conventional art, he did not escape the mimetic conception of art that Lewis

---

3. Ezra Pound, "D'Artagnan Twenty Years After," in *Selected Prose, 1909–1965,* ed. William Cookson (London: Faber & Faber, 1973), p. 454. This article originally appeared in *The Criterion* for July 1937.

4. *Blast,* no. 1 (1914), p. 25.

5. Oscar Wilde, "The Decay of Lying," in *Aesthetes and Decadents of the 1890's,* ed. Karl Beckson (New York: Vintage Books, 1966), p. 169.

was attempting to subvert. His principal targets in *Blast* were the Impressionists (both French and English), who were trying to imitate nature's most delicate effects of light and shade. As befits such a rebel publication as *Blast,* Lewis's attacks were uncompromising ("We want to leave Nature and Men alone") and arrogant ("We are proud, handsome, and predatory. We hunt machines, they are our favorite game"). The somewhat self-mocking passage just cited is from the statement called "Our Vortex," which concludes with a bang:

> Our Vortex rushes out like an angry dog at your Impressionistic fuss.
> Our Vortex is white and abstract with its red-hot swiftness.[6]

Lewis stated his motive for rejecting imitation more carefully when he wrote: "The first reason for not imitating Nature is that you cannot convey the emotion you receive at the contact of Nature by imitating her, but only by becoming her."[7] Painters who tried to give the illusion of the real object would both fail to capture the object and spoil the form of the painting. For example, because the Impressionist tried to imitate the effects of light, "the pigment for its own sake and on its own merits as colour was of no importance."[8] The reality of the painting (its formal qualities) was lost in a vain attempt to create the reality of a natural object. The Vorticists candidly admitted that "WE could not make an Elephant," and so concluded that nature should not be challenged so naively. The Impressionist or Futurist artist, Lewis wrote in *Blast,*

6. Lewis, *Wyndham Lewis on Art,* ed. Walter Michel and C. J. Fox (New York: Funk & Wagnalls, 1969), p. 53.
7. Ibid., p. 73.
8. Ibid., p. 60.

like Narcissus, gets his nose nearer and nearer the surface of Life.

He will get it nipped off if he is not careful, by some Pecksniff-shark sunning its lean belly near the surface, or other lurker beneath his image, who has been feeding on its radiance.

Reality is in the artist, the image only in life. . . .[9]

Lewis's separation of art and life, or art and nature, is echoed by T. S. Eliot: "the difference between art and the event is always absolute."[10] Since the separation is absolute, Lewis believes one can find only a painted equivalent for the event or scene, just as Eliot says that the poet must find an "objective equivalent" or the "formula of that *particular* emotion" he is trying to express.[11] Lewis's summary of his own position is that "the essence of an object is beyond and often in contradiction to, its simple truth. . . . The sense of objects, even, is a sense of the SIGNIFICANCE of the object, and not its avoir-dupois and scientifically ascertainable shapes and perspectives."[12]

How then does the Vorticist capture the "essence" of an object, scene, or emotion? Lewis says that the way to reach this essence is to find the "logic and mathematics" of a scene and re-create them in the "organizing lines and masses of the picture."[13] Similarly, Ezra Pound speaks of creating "lines of force." Pound says that the Vorticist presents a concentrated "image" or "VORTEX . . . a radiant node or cluster."[14] Thus

9. Ibid., p. 38.
10. T. S. Eliot, "Tradition and the Individual Talent," in *Selected Essays* (New York: Harcourt Brace, 1950), p. 9.
11. Eliot, "Hamlet," in ibid., p. 125.
12. *Wyndham Lewis on Art,* p. 74.
13. Ibid., p. 73.
14. Ezra Pound, *Gaudier-Brzeska: A Memoir* (New York: New Directions, 1970), p. 92.

the lines, arcs, and vortices of Lewis's *Timon of Athens* express an image or vortex of the play. Pound says that Lewis's designs are a "creation on the same *motif*" as Shakespeare's play: "That *motif* is the fury of intelligence baffled and shut in by circumjacent stupidity."[15]

Like Lewis, Pound compares the techniques of Vorticist art in reaching the essence of the object to the method of mathematics: "Thus, we learn that the equation $(x - a)^2 + (y - b)^2 = r^2$ governs the circle. It is the circle. It is not a particular circle. . . . It is the circle free of space and time limits."[16] The equation is a generative definition of circles in general rather than a descriptive definition of a particular circle. Pound says that art should also present such an equation (or what Eliot calls a "formula"): "not an equation of mathematics, not something about *a, b,* and *c,* having something to do with form but about *sea, cliffs, night,* having something to do with mood."[17] In a two-page "Vortex" in the 1914 *Blast,* Pound cites as an example of Vorticist poetry a lyric by Hilda Doolittle which illustrates his statement about mathematical form:

> Whirl up, sea—
> whirl your pointed pines,
> splash your great pines
> on our rocks. . . .[18]

The poem does not literally describe a seacoast or explicitly state that a crashing wave resembles a pine tree; instead it juxtaposes images of pines, waves, and rocks. Such starkly presented images Pound calls the "primary pigment" of

15. Ibid., p. 93.
16. Ibid., p. 91.
17. Ibid., p. 92.
18. H. D., "Oread," in *Collected Poems* (New York: Boni & Liveright, 1925), p. 81.

poetry as he asserts that "the Vorticist will not allow the primary expression of any concept or emotion to drag itself out into mimicry."[19] Images are abstracted from the scene and act as equations or formulas for the emotions the artist derives from it. As the Vorticist artist juxtaposes pure form and color, so the Vorticist poet juxtaposes images. The Vorticist differs from the so-called Imagists because he treats images more concisely. Pound wrote to Ford Madox Ford that the "apostacy" of the "Self-styled Imagists" came from their neglect of the rule Pound made when he was an Imagist himself: "To use absolutely no word that does not contribute to the presentation."[20]

Vorticist literary style attempts to avoid this dilution. In addition to "primary pigment," Vorticist style employs abrupt rhythms and parallel constructions (what Lewis called "word-apposition"). One sees this technique in the H. D. poem as well as in the poem Pound himself singled out as being inspired by abstract art.[21] His poem "The Game of Chess" appeared in the 1915 *Blast*:

> Red knights, brown bishops, bright queens,
> Striking the board, falling in strong 'L's of colour.

The purest examples of Vorticist style are found in Lewis's *Enemy of the Stars,* as in this passage concerning the hostile nature of the stars: "Throats iron eternities, drinking heavy radiance, limbs towers of blatant light, the stars poised, immensely distant, with their metal sides, pantheistic machines."[22] The commas measure out what is actually a rough

19. Pound, "Our Vortex," *Blast,* no. 1, p. 154.
20. Pound to Ford Madox Ford, July 30, 1920, Ford Madox Ford Collection, Olin Library, Cornell University.
21. Donald Hall, "Ezra Pound: An Interview," *Paris Review* 28 (Summer–Fall 1962):30.
22. Lewis, *Enemy of the Stars, Blast,* no. 1, p. 64.

verse rhythm. Lewis hated Victorian mellifluousness as much as Pound and believed that stark, jagged rhythms were appropriate to the machine age. We find the same rhythms in Lewis's description of the character who represents the artist's antitype: "Mask of discontent, anxious to explode, restrained by qualms of vanity. . . . Eyes grown venturesome in native temperatures of Pole—indulgent and familiar, blessing with white nights."[23] This rhythm, with its clusters of double and triple stresses culminating in the staccato "white nights," is like Pound's quick rhythms and rapid visual notations in Canto 2:

> Grey peak of the wave,
>> wave, colour of grape's pulp,
> Olive grey in the near,
>> far, smoke grey of the rock-slide.

Pound makes clear his debt to Lewis in the original version of Canto 1, in which the last full lines read:

> Barred lights, great flares, new form, Picasso or Lewis.
> If for a year man write to paint, and not to music—[24]

Even if Lewis were not explicitly mentioned in these lines, the telegraphic style would show the influence of his *Blast* style. And of course the ambition to "write to paint" shows Pound thinking in terms of juxtaposing blocks of material in his *Cantos*—with a freedom from linear development equal to the Vorticist artist's freedom from representational form.

The poems of H. D. and Pound, being of course verbal and referential, were relatively mimetic in comparison with the abstract Vorticist canvases. Even the most advanced poem published in *Blast,* T. S. Eliot's "Preludes," is clearly

23. Ibid., p. 59.
24. Pound, "Three Cantos," *Poetry* 10 (June 1917):121.

mimetic next to a Vorticist design such as Edward Wadsworth's *Newcastle-on-Tyne.*[25] Wadsworth's black-and-white arrangement of jagged, bristling shapes has less to do with Newcastle's appearance than it does with the feelings of power and danger he received from that industrial center. Nevertheless, Eliot does express in "Preludes" a vivid impression of an urban scene through such primary images as "early coffee-stands," "soiled hands," and "blackened street." He avoids the kind of weak, representational technique in which, as Lewis puts it in *Blast,* a "natural scene or person is definitely co-ordinated."[26] Eliot's indefiniteness—who is the woman on the bed in the third "prelude"?—intensifies the poem's sense of desolation. The scene is evoked by images rather than "definitely co-ordinated."[27]

Pound's "Affirmation" of Vorticism in 1915 stressed that "Vorticism means that one is interested in the creative faculty as opposed to the mimetic." He uses his most famous image of the poetic process to illustrate creativity as the Vorticists understand it: "It is only by applying a particular and suitable force that you can bring order and vitality and thence beauty into a plate of iron filings, which are otherwise as 'ugly' as anything under heaven. The design in the magnetised iron filings expresses a confluence of energy." Pound insists that this energy is not related to the "organic," or the "unconscious or sub-human energies or minds of nature"; the Vorticist does not merely assume "the pattern-making faculty which lies in the flower-seed or in the grain or in the animal cell." Instead Vorticism expresses "conscious intellect" and "instinct and intellect together."[28]

25. Wadsworth's woodcut is reproduced in *Blast,* no. 1, p. 29.

26. *Wyndham Lewis on Art,* p. 73.

27. Edward Wadsworth created the designs for Eliot's *Ara Vos Prec* volume of 1920.

28. Pound, "Affirmations. II. Vorticism," *New Age* 16 (January 14, 1915):277–78.

Lewis was not so wary of an analogy between artistic and organic creativity. Although they could use abstract form as the poets could not, the Vorticist artists hesitated to commit themselves entirely to pure abstraction. The antinature passages I have so far quoted from Lewis's criticism in *Blast,* however confident and unequivocal they seem, do not express the whole of his thinking on art, nature, and abstraction. An element of his Vorticist theory is more tolerant of natural forms. This element may appear contradictory at first, but it is really a part of Vorticist dialectic. In a *Blast* manifesto, Lewis writes, "We start from opposite statements of a chosen world. Set up violent structure of adolescent clearness between two extremes."[29] This antithetic naturalism, vague and undeveloped in the pre–World War I period, will become the main theme of Lewis's criticism in the 1920s.

Like the later Russian Constructionists, Vorticists could not consistently maintain that the natural world can be banished from a picture. Lewis the Vorticist scorned the romantic landscapes and city scenes of the English Impressionists and even the apples and mandolins of the Cubists (although Lewis always respected Picasso's genius). Like the Futurists, the Vorticists thought that the artist's subject matter should express the energies of the Machine Age. But did this not lead to imitation of the external world? Lewis argued that it did for the Italian Futurists, who made no advance over the Impressionists by copying speeding automobiles and airplanes rather than flowers and pretty women. The question was whether the Vorticist could avoid this imitative quality. At this point, Lewis was forced to answer that even in the most abstract art there was an "unavoidable representative element."[30] Whether it came from the human

29. *Wyndham Lewis on Art,* p. 27.
30. Ibid., p. 73.

body, machines, clouds, leaves, or the grain of wood, pictorial content could come only from the material world. The crucial requirement for the Vorticist was that he determine the form and not merely take it from nature or rearrange the form given in the external world. The artist must usurp nature's formative power.

The way that the artist takes over nature's function will be clearer if we refer to a work both Lewis and Pound valued highly, Laurence Binyon's introduction to Oriental art, *The Flight of the Dragon* (1911). Pound quoted passages from *The Flight of the Dragon* in *Blast* to support the Vorticist use of rhythm and form for their own sake. A passage that Pound did not quote is basic to Lewis's aesthetic: "It is said that Aristotle did not mean that art imitates the aspect of nature, but the workings of nature. The artist produces his work as the tree produces its fruit."[31] Lewis made a similar distinction, although he applied it in ways that might have disturbed the more conservative Binyon. Lewis said that the great artist has "a perpetually renewed power of DOING WHAT NATURE DOES. . . . Beauty of workmanship in painting and sculpture is the appearance . . . of Growth, the best paintings being in the same category as flowers, insects and animals."[32] However odd or even contradictory it may sound, mechanical images must be arranged in an organic way.

This distinction between imitating nature's appearance and imitating its creative force solved the mimetic problem for Lewis. The creative artist arranges his forms much as the "lines of force" or "moving energies" (Pound's phrases) of the physical universe give form to nature. Laurence Binyon

31. Laurence Binyon, *The Flight of the Dragon* (London: John Murray, 1911), p. 9.
32. *Wyndham Lewis on Art,* pp. 75–76.

again helps to clarify this conception of art in his description of a seventeenth-century Chinese work that was also one of Lewis's artistic touchstones: "You may say that the waves on Korin's famous screen are not like real waves; but they move, they have force and volume. We might in dreams see waves such as these, divested of all accident of appearance, in their naked impetus of movement and recoil."[33] Binyon is seeing the world as a Vorticist would, except that the Vorticist would replace Korin's highly formalized waves with the even more formalized arcs and lines that would make the "impetus of movement and recoil" still more "naked."

Such concepts as imitation and invention, nature and art, imagination and reality, jostled in a chaotic, sometimes contradictory, and always fertile way in Lewis's mind. His thought on these matters was drastically simplified, however, by the events of World War I. To many art historians, Lewis's sudden turn away from abstraction after the war was unfortunate. England now had to wait until the 1930s for Henry Moore and Ben Nicholson to complete the revolution in abstract form. But the turn was inevitable for Lewis.

Lewis said that it was his experience of World War I that disenchanted him from abstraction. He had always regarded painting as the most "inhuman" of the arts. Great art divests man of his "vital plastic qualities," he wrote in *Blast*. "This dehumanizing has corresponded happily with the unhuman character, the plastic, architectural quality, of art itself."[34] Wyndham Lewis the Vorticist wanted to accentuate this dehumanization, but Lewis the artillery officer was repelled when he saw in the "hideous desert known as 'the Line' in Flanders and France . . . a subject matter so consonant with

33. Binyon, *Flight of the Dragon,* p. 17.
34. *Wyndham Lewis on Art,* p. 70.

the austerity of that 'abstract' vision": "when Mars with his mailed finger showed me a shell crater and a skeleton, with a couple of shivered tree stumps behind it, I was still in my 'abstract' element. And before I knew quite what I was doing I was drawing with loving care a signaler corporal to plant upon the lip of the shell crater."[35]

It was grimly symbolic that Lewis's old friend and colleague T. E. Hulme, the antihumanist who praised the geometric at the expense of the vital qualities of art, was killed not far from Lewis's gun pit. Lewis emerged from the war a committed humanist who would ask why any artist "would paint a tree when he could paint a man."[36] Lewis announced his about-face at the exhibition ("Guns," 1919) of his works as an official war artist: "The public, surprised at finding eyes and noses in this exhibition, will begin by the reflection that the artist has conceded Nature, and abandoned those vexing diagrams by which he puzzled and annoyed. The case is really not quite that." He explained that he still remained faithful to Vorticism's emphasis on the "fundamentals of design or colour."[37] But Lewis was clearly ready to make his peace with representational form. Ezra Pound was not.

Pound wrote two separate reviews of the "Guns" exhibition. Although he praised Lewis's pictures of gun pits and wounded men as "the most thoughtful exposition of the war that any painter has yet given us," he also announced that "I give up no jot of my admiration, of my preference for his 'abstract' work."[38] He had a similar preference for the more

35. Lewis, *Rude Assignment: A Narrative of My Career Up-to-Date* (London: Hutchinson, 1950), p. 128.
36. *Wyndham Lewis on Art,* p. 331.
37. Ibid., p. 104.
38. Pound, "War Paintings by Wyndham Lewis," *The Nation,* February 8, 1919, pp. 546–47. The second review of this show appeared in *The New Age* and is reprinted in Pound's *Selected Prose.*

abstract work of Henri Gaudier. When Pound published his
memoir of Gaudier in 1915, he praised his more abstract
work over his representational sculptures. Gaudier's naturalistic *Dancer* and marble torsos were virtually ignored as
Pound praised such Vorticist works as *Red Stone Dancer*. He
disapproved of the sentiment Gaudier expressed when writing from the trenches about a naturalistic work he had
carved: "I am getting convinced slowly that it is not much
use going farther in the research of planes, forms, etc. If I
ever come back I shall do more 'Mlles. G. . . .' in marble."[39]
The war seems to have turned Gaudier, as it did Wyndham
Lewis, from his abstract vision. Pound was clearly distressed
when he footnoted the Gaudier passage just quoted: "'Mlle.
G. . . .' is the nickname of a naturalistic torse. . . . He had
repeatedly stigmatised it as insincere. However, this passage
is all that I can find about the 'renunciation' so vaunted by
our enemies."[40] Although Gaudier never "renounced" Vorticism, even in 1914 he was turning from Vorticist abstraction
toward more naturalistic, organic forms. The clearest sign of
Pound's preferences after the war was his interest in the
abstract artists Francis Picabia and Constantin Brancusi. In
1921 he wrote that "Brancusi was giving up the facile success
of representative sculpture about the time Gaudier was
giving up his baby bottle."[41]

During the twenties, Wyndham Lewis worked in both
abstract and representational styles. His main ambition was
to synthesize what he now called "Nature and Design" in his
portraits. A rather severe formalism ruled in such pictures as
his geometric treatment of Edith Sitwell in 1923 (Fig. 11).
But this severity and the icy, silent quality of the portrait's

39. Pound, *Gaudier-Brzeska,* p. 68.
40. Ibid.
41. Pound, "Brancusi," in *Literary Essays of Ezra Pound* (New York:
New Directions, 1968), p. 442.

11. Wyndham Lewis, *Edith Sitwell*. The Tate Gallery, London.

greens, blues, and grays suit Lewis's judgment on Edith Sitwell's artistic superficiality. Although a recent critic has praised the Sitwell portrait as perhaps Lewis's best, he thinks that its iconography of books to suggest the writer's vocation fails to work because Sitwell's "hieratic figure is so strange and impassive."[42] This impassivity is really Lewis's point; Sitwell is as cut off from genuine literature as the bright, metallic colors of her garments are from the warm browns of the books. Her pale, abstracted face seems isolated from its surroundings. Remarkably, Lewis expresses his sense of Sitwell as a failed artist, a priestess without a cult, while still acknowledging her dignity and self-assurance. He achieves this mixture of censure and sympathy through the great care of his draftsmanship, as in the contours of Sitwell's fragile nose, mouth, and chin. Although his drawings are more studied than Gaudier's, they can also reveal a character in a few lines. Gaudier would astonish his classmates by producing more than one hundred vivid sketches in a two- or three-hour session, and an observer of Lewis's methods noted that his ink drawings used no preliminary sketches or any scaffolding in pencil.[43] If either Gaudier or Lewis failed to capture the image he wanted, he would simply discard his mistakes and start again. Lewis's line, however, unlike Gaudier's, always has a spring and snap to it that produces a harsher and more exciting effect. Even a playful pencil sketch such as *The Duc de Joyeux Sings* (Fig. 12), which mocks Joyce's claims to noble descent, uses a violent stream

42. Robin Gibson, *Twentieth-Century Portraits: Exhibition at 15 Carlton House Terrace* (London: National Portrait Gallery, 1978), p. 43. Both the Sitwell and the Pound portraits are reproduced in color in Walter Michel's *Wyndham Lewis: Paintings and Drawings* (Berkeley and Los Angeles: University of California Press, 1971).

43. Charles Handley-Read, "Detail in the Style of Wyndham Lewis," in *The Art of Wyndham Lewis* (London: Faber & Faber, 1951), p. 59.

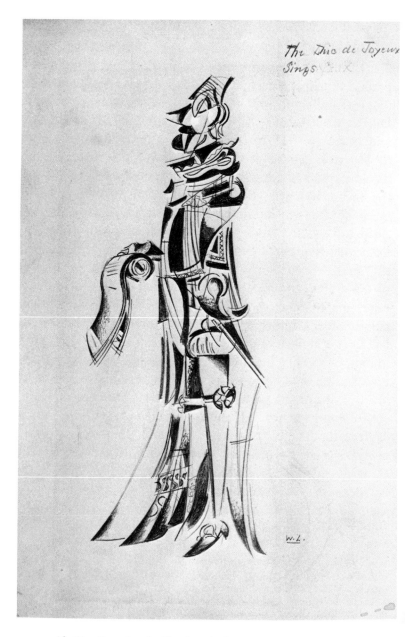

12. Wyndham Lewis, *The Duc de Joyeux Sings.* Walter Michel.

122

of arcs and angles to suggest the élan of Joyce's character. Every unit of the sketch is energized, from the springlike manuscript to the vortical garter to the sweep of the full-length cloak. One sees this "whiplash" quality of Lewis's drawings in the curves of Pound's Byronic shirt collar (Fig. 13), in the thrust of Eliot's head (Fig. 14), even in the coil of the newspaper in the portrait of Ezra Pound (Fig. 15).[44] The drawing of Eliot conveys the poet's nerve and strength in the lines of the nose, the slitted eyes, and the wary loop of the left eyebrow. Eliot's cylindrical, starched collar, in contrast to Pound's open-necked shirt, suggests constraint or even repression while at the same time accenting the power of his neck and shoulders. The nearly solid rectangle of Pound's forehead (Fig. 13) conveys his fanatical willpower. In the drawings of Eliot and Pound, sharp geometric forms express the artist's creative force.

As he attempted to alleviate the "inhuman" structural quality of visual art, Lewis created warmer and less geometric portraits than the one of Sitwell. He came to realize that it took "as much skill and resource to keep design and significance on the Nature side of the cleavage as it does to keep vitality and objective truth on the side of Design."[45] Lewis achieved this synthesis of nature and design in the works most critics consider his masterpieces, such portraits of the 1930s as those of Ezra Pound and T. S. Eliot.

Lewis painted the Pound portrait in 1939, when Pound was briefly in London to dispose of his mother-in-law's apartment after her death, a task he accomplished in part by giving away the furniture to such friends as Lewis. Lewis recalled that Pound would arrive for a sitting with "coattails

44. On Lewis's "whiplash" quality, see Eric Newton, "Wyndham Lewis," in Art of Wyndham Lewis, ed. Handley-Read, p. 25.
45. Wyndham Lewis on Art, p. 125.

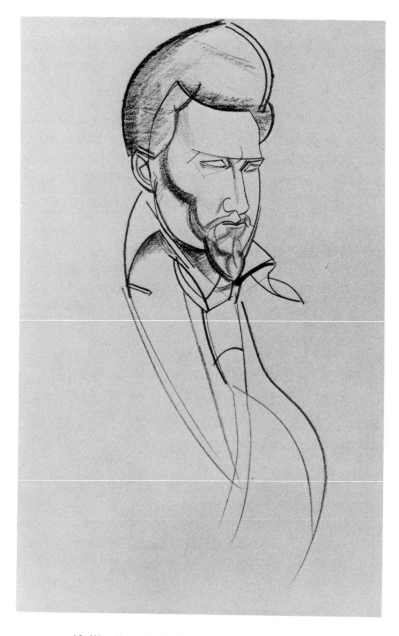

13. Wyndham Lewis, *Ezra Pound*. Anthony d'Offay.

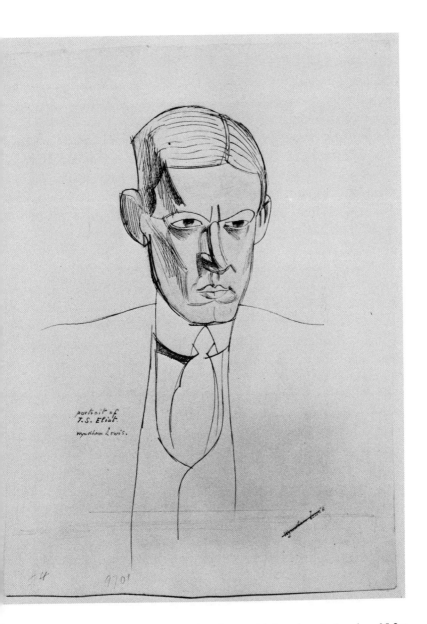

4. Wyndham Lewis, *Portrait of T. S. Eliot.* Pen and ink and wash drawing, 35.2 ×
5.4 cm. Felton Bequest, 1950. Reproduced by permission of the National Gallery
f Victoria, Melbourne.

15. Wyndham Lewis, *Ezra Pound*. The Tate Gallery, London.

flying, a malacca cane out of the Nineties aslant beneath his arm, the lion's head . . . thrown back."[46] Pound would throw himself in a chair, not asleep but exhausted and motionless, for a two-hour sitting. The portrait observes him in this pose, with his eyes closed and his "lion's head" pressed against the chair's back. The diagonal design of the poet's form, against the marine-like, horizontal background, coheres with a sharp but sympathetic reading of Pound as an unquiet dreamer. The background colors are a misty pale green, orange, and pink; and Pound's body and hands are dissolved in a rush of dark pigment. Emphasis falls on the sculptural density of the poet's head and suggests a mind/body duality that is characteristic of Lewis's work. There is a similar contrast of head and body in the 1938 Eliot portrait, in which Eliot's figure is encased in a correct and conservative lounge suit but his "skull beneath the skin" is sharply focused. With his great portraits behind him, Lewis made a classic statement of his artistic principles:

Today I am a *super-naturalist*—so I might call myself: and I wished [the public] to see what could be done by burying Euclid deep in the living flesh—that of Mr. Eliot or of Mr. Pound—rather than . . . displaying the astral geometries of those gentlemen. I am . . . never unconscious of those underlying conceptual truths that are inherent in all appearances. But I leave them now where I find them, instead of isolating them in conceptual arabesques.[47]

This statement does not mean that Lewis was imitating nature by providing accurate images of Eliot and Pound.

46. Lewis, "Early London Environment," in *T. S. Eliot: A Collection of Critical Essays,* ed. Hugh Kenner (Englewood Cliffs, N.J.: Prentice-Hall, 1962), p. 32.
47. *Wyndham Lewis on Art,* p. 330.

He was not trying to bring his sitters to life through tricks of perspective or lighting. Indeed, the paint on the Ezra Pound portrait is so thin that it accents the physical reality of the canvas. Lewis was presenting painted equivalents of his sitters in which the latent organization of their forms stands forth. This organization is not imposed, in the Vorticist manner, but discovered.

Lewis's "super-naturalism" was supported by his readings in scientific naturalism, especially in the works of a pioneer of entomology, Henri Fabre. Here again Pound and Lewis converged as their interest in the natural world deepened. Pound's interest in natural history had developed at least by 1922, when he translated Remy de Gourmont's *Natural Philosophy of Love.* Gourmont studied animal and insect behavior to show that no "natural law" supports sexual customs. Although Gourmont's method was utterly unscientific, he did gather some fascinating natural history—much of it from Henri Fabre, whom Pound declared to be "essential to contemporary clear thinking."[48] Lewis also admired Fabre's close observation of reality. Early in his career he wrote, "Henri Fabre was in every way a superior being to a Salon artist, and he knew of elegant grubs which he would prefer to the Salon painter's nymphs."[49] Lewis wrote some of the greatest satire in modern fiction (particularly in the 1930 *Apes of God*) on the principle of closely observing the speech and mannerisms of upper-class dilettantes. He considered his satire a kind of documentary: his accurate recording of the social life of the twenties is both realism and satire. Pound admired *The Apes of God* for its documentary

48. Pound, *Literary Essays,* p. 32.
49. Lewis, *The Wild Body: A Soldier of Humour and Other Stories* (London: Chatto & Windus, 1928), p. 242. An unpublished essay on Fabre is among Lewis's papers in the Olin Library, Cornell University.

quality, as well as two other books he classed with it, Joyce's
Ulysses and E. E. Cummings's *Eimi*. He wrote that the events
recorded in *The Apes* "diagnose a state of society, which has
led to the present conflict [World War II]."[50] Pound's own
reliance on documentation is evident in the Malatesta
Cantos (1923), with their use of letters and official documents drawn from the life of the Renaissance *condottiere*
Sigismundo Malatesta. A documentary quality then characterizes all of the cantos with the exception of the Pisan
sequence and the Fragments. Just as significant is his
increasingly careful and detailed method of describing nature.

As a poet Pound was never so "abstract" ("rotten bad
word 'abstract' in this connection," he told John Quinn) that
he banished external nature from his poetry. Although he
detested romantic "nature" poetry, an idyllic vision of nature
runs through his poetry from his earliest lyrics until the last
cantos. In his early poetry nature imagery is used convention-
ally; as Lewis observed, there is a "stage-property" quality
about it. This quality is strong up until the China Cantos
(52-61), as in the lush imagery of Canto 39:

> with sap new in the bough
> With plum flowers above them
> with almond on the black bough
> With jasmine and olive leaf . . .

Even the fine nature imagery of Canto 47 ("forked boughs
shake with the wind") and of Canto 49 ("flowing water clots
as with cold") is relatively subjective compared to that of his
later poetry. Nature is wholly absorbed into the poet's

50. Pound, "Argument of the Novel," in *New Directions in Prose and Poetry, 1941* (Norfolk, Conn.: New Directions, 1941), p. 710.

consciousness and often for the purpose of symbolizing his personal sense of spiritual renewal.

The use of nature in the first of the China Cantos, on the other hand, is direct and impersonal:

> This month are trees in full sap
> Rain has now drenched all the earth
> > dead weeds enrich it, as if boil'd in a bouillon. . . .
> > cold wind is beginning. Dew whitens.
> Now is cicada's time,
> > The sparrow hawk offers birds to the spirits.

In this passage, which is based on the Confucian *Li Chi,* or *Book of Rites,* Pound has abandoned his own personality to a reality beyond it. Natural renewal is not limited to the poet or to one of his personae. Pound's method of describing external scenes in such passages, as opposed to W. B. Yeats's or T. S. Eliot's, has been distinguished by Donald Davie. He writes that Pound's landscapes are characterized by the "discipline that is the scientist's as much as the artist's, exact and intent observation."[51] (Wyndham Lewis cited Leonardo da Vinci as the classic figure in this tradition.) Davie observes that Pound is not often considered in terms of a "reverent vigilance before the natural world" or "the habit of the biologist . . . partly because these are not the terms in which he talks of himself."[52] Yet in the *Rock-Drill* cantos (1955) Pound praises the seventeenth-century "Secretary of Nature, J[ohn] Heydon," and the nineteenth-century American naturalist Louis Agassiz. And in *Thrones* (1959) Linnaeus and the American anthropologist Joseph Rock, as well as Agassiz, are major figures in Pound's *paradisio.*

51. Donald Davie, *Ezra Pound: Poet as Sculptor* (New York: Oxford University Press, 1964), p. 174.
52. Ibid., p. 177.

In a letter to Lewis in the fifties, Pound wrote that "fer CONservatives, there is a SANE tradition, to be found in Mencius, Ocellus . . . Dante AND Agassiz."[53] Pound describes these thinkers in terms similar to those used by Lewis in describing the creative power of the artist. He tells Lewis, "a Solid core lasts through the lot/ respect for the KIND of intelligence that enables cherry stone to grow cherries/"[54] This tradition is invoked in Canto 113, where Agassiz and Linnaeus appear in a context related to Joseph Rock's descriptions of the Na-khi landscape of Southwest China:

> Yet to walk with Mozart, Agassiz and Linnaeus
>   'neath overhanging air under sun-beat . . .
> And over Li Chiang, the snow range is turquoise
> Rock's world that he saved us for memory
>   a thin trace in high air . . .

Rock's precise descriptions are a major source for what Carroll Terrell calls Pound's "landscape of Paradise" in lines like these from Canto 101: "Mint grows at the foot of the Snow Range / the first moon is the tiger's, / Pheasant calls out of bracken . . ."[55] Canto 106 contains a superb example of an impersonal rendering of external nature:

> Gold light, in veined phyllotaxis.
> By hundred blue-gray over their rock-pool,
>   Or the king-wings in migration
>   And in thy mind beauty, O Artemis
> Over asphodel, over broom-plant . . .

Canto 106 concerns the way the processes of nature are related to the pagan gods. The gold of wheat sheaves and the

---

53. Pound to Lewis, n.d. (sent from St. Elizabeths Hospital in the 1950s), Olin Library, Cornell University.
54. Pound to Lewis, c. 1951, Olin Library, Cornell University.
55. See Carroll F. Terrell, "The Na-Khi Documents I: The Landscape of Paradise," *Paideuma* 3 (Spring 1974):90–122.

blue-gray of pines, as well as the birds and plants, are one with Artemis, goddess of the moon and so of natural cycles. The words "mind beauty" refer to the kind of creative intelligence found in nature, as in the phyllotaxis or pattern of leaves. Pound has moved far from his 1915 wariness of the "sub-human energies" of nature. This distance is also measured by his praise for Laurence Binyon and Gaudier in the late cantos. In Canto 87 he recalls "BinBin's" statement that "'Slowness is beauty'" in a passage on the slowness of organic growth: "pine seed splitting cliff's edge. / Only sequoias are slow enough." In Canto 107 he praises both Gaudier and Agassiz for their "persistent awareness" of nature's power. Pound now remembers Gaudier as the creator of the same "naturalistic torse" that he criticized in 1915 as a departure from Vorticist principles.[56] He refers to this torso and two other works by the name of Gaudier's model for them, Nina Hamnet, and contrasts Gaudier's "awareness" to the blindness of contemporary man:

> this persistent awareness
> Three Ninas from Gaudier,
>> Their mania is a lusting for farness
>> Blind to the olive leaf,
>> not seeing the oak's veins.

Pound's and Lewis's departure from the severe standards of Vorticism is evident in the imagery of Lewis's prose and Pound's poetry. In *The Human Age* (1955), Lewis imagines a ruler who is as powerful as the one he dreamed of in *The Caliph's Design* (1919). But Lewis now presents this ruler's Vorticist designs as cold and sinister. In the dictator's recep-

56. See my "Henri Gaudier's 'Three Ninas,'" *Paideuma* 4 (Fall and Winter 1975):323–24. A "Nina" that Pound owned is pictured on Plate XIV of Pound's *Gaudier-Brzeska*. See also *Gaudier-Brzeska*, p. 146.

tion room "the plants . . . had no flowers: their greens were
all of the cactus type, preferring a desertic green, bordering
on blue: and geometric designs in white representing glittering flowers."[57] Lewis's protagonist in *The Human Age*
finally understands the sterility of this mechanistic environment when he looks, as if for the first time, at a real flower:
"It seemed to him miraculously beautiful. It came from the
Far-East of the Earth. There physical beauty was understood. The European believed he had evolved spiritual
beauty of a high order—but did the spiritual product ever
come up to this physical perfection?"[58]

The vortex appears in Pound's late cantos in subtly varied
organic forms, such as a "rose in the steel dust" (Canto 74)
and "as a leaf borne in the current" (Canto 80). In the image
of a leaf in a current, Pound reverts to the Greek basis of the
word vortex (*dine*), which was a whirlpool or eddy in wind or
water,[59] as again in the line "the jade weathers dust-swirl"
(Canto 104), and in this appearance of Cythera in Canto 91:

> Rose, azure,
>   the lights slow moving round her,
> Zephyrus, turning,
>   the petals light on the air.

In Canto 100 the spiritual energy of the vortex lifts the poet

> Out of Erebus
> Where no mind moves at all.
>   In crystal funnel of air. . . .

Both the funnel, or vortex, image and the image of crystal
have their source in a work that Pound read before 1914,

57. Lewis, *The Human Age* (London: Methuen, 1955), p. 122.
58. Ibid., p. 560.
59. See John Burnet, *Early Greek Philosophy* (New York: Meridian
Books, 1957), p. 61.

Allen Upward's *New Word* (1908). Upward speaks of "knowledge flowing in on him from all sides" just as Pound speaks of the "VORTEX, from which, and through which, and into which, ideas are constantly rushing." Upward says that in this experience, "Those vortices of Descartes, those whirl-rings in the ether, all seemed to come together and to blend in the ball which I thought that I had shaped."[60] He then shows that this ball, rather like the sea in Pound's "Portrait d'une Femme," is greater than any personal thought: "It is a magic crystal, and by looking long into it, you will see wonderful meanings come and go. . . . It is a most chameleon-like ball. It has this deeper magic that it will show you, not only the thoughts you knew about before, but other thoughts you did not know of, old, drowned thoughts, hereditary thoughts."[61] The vortex of thought solidifies into a crystal, a magically changing and growing object, "feeding upon the earth-strength, and sending it forth in roots and shoots."[62] Pound writes in Canto 116:

> I have brought the great ball of crystal;
> who can lift it?

Pound and Lewis made final statements of their views of the artist's relationship with nature in introductions to picture catalogs in 1956. In his introduction to a small book of Sherri Martinelli's paintings, Pound stated that Lewis and Picasso had revived the sense of form in modern painting. Unfortunately, an "era of technique" followed their innovations: "As with 'vers libre', so with what was called 'abstract' painting, hundreds of crab lice or potato bugs crawled over

60. Allen Upward, *The New Word* (London: A. C. Fifield, 1908), pp. 182–83.
61. Ibid., p. 197.
62. Ibid., p. 198.

the small amount of painting which had revived the sense of occidental composition."[63] Lewis's preface to his own Tate Gallery exhibition, "Wyndham Lewis and Vorticism," also complained about the development of abstract art. He asserted that "finally, I am sure that, in one form or another, Nature supplies us with all we need."[64]

Pound recommended his Martinelli introduction to Lewis and compared it to Lewis's own preface, which Pound called "one of best statements yu hv/ ever made. I dunno whether yu note convergence . . . on agreement of 1913 or whenever. At any rate there was a convergence not merely a connection."[65] The convergence was of course on the belief that, in Lewis's words, "Nature supplies us with all we need," and in the words of Pound quoted at the beginning of this chapter, that Vorticism means an "understanding of basic forms, both in natr/ and ON the kanVASS." The results of this convergence were such great Lewis portraits as his *Ezra Pound* and the landscapes of the late cantos.

63. Pound, "Introduction," *La Martinelli*; reprinted *Edge,* October 1956, n.p.
64. *Wyndham Lewis on Art,* p. 453.
65. Pound to Lewis, "5 or 6 Oc/" 1956, Olin Library, Cornell University.

5

Abstract Entities

> For wherein does the realism of mankind properly consist? In
> the assertion that there exists a something without them, what,
> or how, or where they know not, which occasions the objects of
> their perceptions? Oh no!
>
> —S. T. Coleridge

"God's eye art'ou, do not surrender perception," Ezra
Pound wrote in Canto 113. This warning was still needed
more than a century after William Wordsworth and Samuel
Taylor Coleridge expounded the creativity of the human
mind. The modern artist continued to oppose the belief that
the "real" world was the abstract one of the physical
sciences. W. B. Yeats said that the "mischief" began when
John Locke "separated the primary and secondary qualities;
and from that day to this the conception of a physical world
without colour, sound, taste, tangibility . . . has remained
the assumption of science, the ground-work of every text-
book."[1] Yeats and Pound demonstrated the mind's participa-
tion in the reality of the sensuous world as Wordsworth and
John Keats had in the nineteenth century. T. S. Eliot and
Wyndham Lewis also challenged, as Coleridge had done in
his time, the scientists and philosophers of science on their
own ground. Eliot and Lewis believed that the "mischief"
sprang from narrow, verbalistic definitions of reality. Eliot's
criticism is explicit in his Harvard doctoral dissertation and

1. W. B. Yeats, "Bishop Berkeley," in *Essays and Introductions* (New
York: Collier, 1961), p. 401.

implicit in his prose throughout his career as well as in the poetry of *Four Quartets*. Less cautious and exact than Eliot, Lewis in *Time and Western Man* (1927) attacked such philosopher-scientists as Bertrand Russell and Alfred North Whitehead for the terms they used to describe the phenomenal world. Pound, on the other hand, merely expressed his contempt for such a "flat-chested highbrow" as Russell.[2] Although Pound, Eliot, and Lewis agreed on the nature of the mischief, their techniques of dealing with it were highly personal.

Pound distrusted formal religion and philosophy because they encouraged contemplation rather than action. He wrote that "to replace the marble goddess on her pedestal at Terracina is worth more than any metaphysical argument."[3] Late in his life, he summed up his attitude toward religious belief in a letter to Lewis (in the following, "grampaw" is Pound himself, "Bugson" Henri Bergson, and "Possum" Eliot): "Grampaw believed in horse-sense while the Bugsons, Possums etc/ were chasing fads, and pipple trying to find something they COULD believe in instead of gitting down to what one CAN believe."[4] Like Samuel Johnson when he dismissed Bishop Berkeley's immaterialism by kicking a rock ("I refute him thus"), Pound rejected speculations that seemed to him morally inconclusive. In the *Criterion* he inveighed against "Berkeleyian-Bergsonian subjectivo-fluxivity."[5] As the author of the *Rock-Drill* cantos, Pound attacked

2. Ezra Pound, *Guide to Kulchur* (New York: New Directions, 1968), p. 166.

3. Ezra Pound, *Selected Prose, 1909–1965,* ed. William Cookson (New York: New Directions, 1968), p. 45.

4. Pound to Lewis, n.d. (sent from St. Elizabeths), Olin Library, Cornell University.

5. Ezra Pound, "Epstein, Belgion, and Meaning," *Criterion* 9 (April 1930):474.

the bedrock of reality with a pneumatic drill rather than a Johnsonian boot. But behind the aggressive and violent convictions of Ezra Pound was a concern with practical morality equal to Sam Johnson's.

Nevertheless, Pound had an implicit metaphysics of his own which was rooted in religious perceptions. He never examined his perceptions with Eliot's professional expertise; nor did he subject them to the test of comparative analysis, as Lewis tested his ideas in *Time and Western Man.* From his earliest lyrics to his last cantos, Pound instead passionately asserts a belief in the universe as a system of energies that is unified at some mysterious point or "node." The artist's place is at the still center of this energy vortex, or at this node of organic development. We have seen in Chapter 4 that he speaks in the 1908 poem "Plotinus," "As one that would draw through the node of things, / Back-sweeping to the vortex of the cone," and that in one of the final cantos he envisions "the great acorn of light." In another early poem, he writes of a Mediterranean landscape:

> Sapphire Benacus, in thy mists and thee
> Nature herself's turned metaphysical,
> Who can look on that blue and not believe?[6]

To a passage such as this, Eliot might well ask, as he once did in another context, "What does Mr. Pound believe?" The nature of a faith derived from dwelling on "metaphysical" scenery is certainly vague. But this belief is explored if not analyzed in Pound's early criticism and poetry.

In "Plotinus" Pound does not claim that he has shared Plotinus's experience of the "node" or "vortex" of the

6. Ezra Pound, "The Flame," in *Personae* (New York: New Directions, 1971), p. 50.

universe. Yet the assumption implicit in his verse collection *Personae* (1909) is that the poet expands his awareness of the universe by absorbing the experience of great poets and thinkers. The "Plotinus" poem is an example of this process. Faced with the "utter loneliness" of his mystical perceptions, Pound's persona says that he makes further images, or personae, of himself:

> And then for utter loneliness, made I
> New thoughts as crescent images of *me*.
> And with them was my essence reconciled. . . .[7]

Pound seems to comment on this poem when he explains his "search for the real" in his early poetry:

> One says "I am" this, that, or the other, and with the words scarcely uttered one ceases to be that thing.
> I began this search for the real in a book called *Personae,* casting off, as it were, complete masks of the self in each poem.[8]

The poetic mind that Pound explores through such personae as Plotinus is described in his well-known chapter "Psychology and the Troubadours" in *The Spirit of Romance*. There Pound says that the consciousness of the poet is an organic force; his thoughts are like seeds: "they affect mind about them, and transmute it as the seed the earth." Because the poet's mind is one with the "germinal universe," he can perceive the ultimate reality of the "universe of fluid force."[9] These "fluid forces" may assume the shape of a vortex, or of a rose pattern such as a magnet may enforce in

7. Ezra Pound, "Plotinus," in *A Lume Spento and Other Early Poems* (New York: New Directions, 1965), p. 56.

8. Ezra Pound, *Gaudier-Brzeska: A Memoir* (New York: New Directions, 1970), p. 85.

9. Ezra Pound, *The Spirit of Romance* (New York: New Directions, 1968), pp. 93, 92.

metallic dust. The poet perceives such shapes, unlike the scientist, for whom "energy has no borders, it is a shapeless 'mass' of force."[10] Moreover, the mind does not merely perceive. There are two ways of thinking about man in relation to experience: "Firstly, you may think of him as that toward which perception moves . . . as the plastic substance *receiving* impressions; secondly, you may think of him as directing a certain fluid force against circumstance, as *conceiving* instead of merely reflecting and observing."[11] The "fluid force" within matches the physical forces without and creates the forms by which we apprehend our experiences.

Pound struggled to relate his conception of a fluid universe to his poetic language in 1910, when he described words as "great hollow cones of steel . . . charged with a force like electricity, or, rather, radiating forces from their apexes."[12] The cones are like the vortices of a period two and one half years later. In 1913 he discovered in Ernest Fenollosa's *Chinese Written Character* a theory of language that confirmed his intuitions. Fenollosa said that the sentence ideally gives "a vivid shorthand picture of the operations of nature" and that these operations reveal the "transferences of forces from agent to object, which constitutes natural phenomena."[13] It follows that accurate writing should rely on active verbs. In a famous passage, Fenollosa writes: "A true noun, an isolated thing, does not exist in nature. Things are only the terminal points, or rather the meeting points, of actions, cross-sections cut through actions, snapshots."[14] As

10. Pound, *Literary Essays of Ezra Pound* (New York: New Directions, 1968), p. 154.
11. Pound, *Gaudier-Brzeska,* p. 89.
12. Pound, *Selected Prose,* p. 34.
13. Ernest Fenollosa, *The Chinese Written Character as a Medium for Poetry,* ed. Ezra Pound (San Francisco: City Lights Books, 1969), pp. 8, 7.
14. Ibid., p. 10.

Hugh Kenner points out, this passage recalls Pound's conception of a "VORTEX, from which, and through which, and into which, ideas are constantly rushing."[15]

In Pound's touchstone for Vorticist poetry, H. D.'s "Oread," images of waves and pine branches are yoked by the single verb "splash": "Splash your great pines / On our rocks . . ." The verb infuses H. D.'s mental energy into the poem. In the original 1917 version of Canto 1, Pound shows how Robert Browning breathed his own life into his persona Sordello and gave form to Sordello's world:

> what were the use
> Of setting figures up and breathing life upon them,
> Weren't not *our* life, your life, my life, extended?

As Browning created a whole world in *Sordello,* so Pound's Cantos will discover

> the new world about us:
> Barred lights, great flares, new form, Picasso or Lewis.[16]

Herbert Schneidau writes of Pound's "deep and almost naive faith in the powers of language to coalesce with reality." Schneidau shows that Fenollosa opened for Pound "a way across the terrifying Cartesian gap between internal and external, between subjective and objective"—a way opened through a poetic language capable of controlling the fluid forces of reality.[17] Although Pound was no more naive than Sam Johnson, he does assume an order within reality knowable by man. He chose not to look down into the

15. Pound, *Gaudier-Brzeska,* p. 92.
16. Pound, "Three Cantos," I, *Poetry* 10 (June 1917):115, 121.
17. Herbert N. Schneidau, *Ezra Pound: The Image and the Real* (Baton Rouge: Louisiana State University Press, 1969), pp. 51–52, 61.

Cartesian gap the better to keep his balance. Hence such assertions, "naive" but necessary to his mission as a poet, as "An *image,* in our sense, is real because we know it directly."[18] Pound operated out of what he called "Axiomata": for example, "The universe exists. By exists we mean normally: is perceptible to our consciousness or deducible by human reason from data perceptible to our consciousness."[19] Such an axiom cuts through a great deal of rock. Late in his career, Pound returned to the Cartesian problem even more audaciously. In *The Pisan Cantos* he revises the Cartesian *cogito:* "Amo ergo sum, and in just that proportion" (Canto 80). Perception, or what he might call conception, must be an activity of our whole selves and is dependent upon our power to love. Otherwise we cannot grasp—certainly not through abstract thought—the nature of reality, Pound writes in Canto 90, which meditates on Richard of St. Victor's insight that love is the essential function of the human soul, "UBI AMOR IBI OCULUS EST." Where love is, there is the eye—creative perception. It exerts its fluid force. Pound expressed his mature convictions on these matters at the conclusion of the first Pisan canto in the only way it can be expressed for him, in lines of great poetry:

> Serenely in the crystal jet
> > as the bright ball that the fountain tosses . . .
> > out of hell, the pit
> > out of the dust and glare evil . . .
> This liquid is certainly a
> > property of the mind . . .
> est agens and functions dust to a fountain pan otherwise
> > Hast 'ou seen the rose in the steel dust . . .?

18. Pound, *Gaudier-Brzeska,* p. 86.
19. *Selected Prose,* p. 49.

In 1928 Pound recalled Eliot's philosophical orientation as "a general belief that one should not in the matter of basic ideas have a pup sold to one." [20] Eliot's skeptical wariness of such basic ideas developed when he wrote his doctoral dissertation. He completed this work, *Knowledge and Experience in the Philosophy of F. H. Bradley,* in 1916. Whether one thinks of the Lockean distinction of primary and secondary qualities or the Cartesian duality of consciousness and its objects, the seeming dualities of experience cause endless philosophical confusions. Eliot's modest goal in his dissertation is to clarify some typical problems that arise from false dichotomies. "In the theory which I outline," he writes, "the distinction of objective and subjective, external reality and mental, is unnecessary." [21] Eliot's critics assume that he is in the Idealist camp. Yet the terms "real" and "ideal," much less "Realist" and "Idealist," are far from clear, and "the apparently fundamental separation between the real and the ideal is but tentative and provisional, a moment in a process." [22] Eliot writes as a critic, however sympathetic, rather than as a proponent of Bradley's idealism, and he could have sympathized with Lewis's feeling that "'idealist' is to-day a meaningless and, by association, semi-idiotic word." [23] One must therefore pay special attention to Eliot's terminology.

Most commentators on Eliot's dissertation concentrate on the subject of its first chapter—the treatment of what Bradley calls "immediate experience," which is "reality"

20. Pound, "Data," *Exile,* Autumn 1928, p. 107.
21. T. S. Eliot, *Knowledge and Experience in the Philosophy of F. H. Bradley* (London: Faber & Faber, 1964), p. 126.
22. Ibid., p. 32.
23. Wyndham Lewis, *Time and Western Man* (London: Chatto & Windus, 1927), p. 254.

before it is categorized by the mind. A second major concern is Bradley's ultimate reality, the "Absolute Experience." Eliot himself is far more interested in immediate experience, which is a partial but direct perception of the world, than in Absolute Experience, which is a total but merely inferred perception of the world. Critics of the dissertation generally conclude that Eliot's treatment of these topics expresses a despairing attitude. George Whiteside, who has written the most detailed and useful study of the dissertation, says that Eliot despairs because he cannot believe that Bradley's Absolute exists; and most critics of *The Waste Land* interpret the citation of Bradley in the poem's notes as an "endorsement" (to use Whiteside's word) of Bradley's alleged solipsism.[24] Nevertheless, the tone of the dissertation is quite positive. It resembles the self-assured tone of Eliot's first book of criticism, *The Sacred Wood* (1920), in which epigrammatic assertiveness at times stops just short of arrogance. For example, in *Knowledge and Experience,* Eliot delivers the following judgment on reason and emotion: "There is no greater mistake than to think that feeling and thought are exclusive—that those beings which think most and best are not also those capable of the most feeling" (p. 18). If this remark seems unusually confident for an academic thesis, the following is indeed daring for the concluding pages of a philosophical work: "Metaphysical systems are condemned to go up like a rocket and come down like a stick" (p. 168). Even these remarks pale beside his declaration about the subject of his first chapter: "If anyone assert that immediate experience . . . is annihilation and utter night, I cordially agree" (p. 31).

Despite the jaunty tone of that remark, both George

24. George Whiteside, "T. S. Eliot's Dissertation," *English Literary History* 34 (September 1967):421.

Whiteside and Lyndall Gordon discover in it the despair they also find in such early Eliot poems as "Preludes." This despair arises because Eliot, unlike Bradley, cannot believe that the Absolute Experience guarantees that immediate experience really is a whole. As Whiteside says, "To embrace Bradleian monism yet feel obliged to reject its ultimate underpinning, as Eliot apparently did, led him, I think, to despair." [25] There is an obvious problem here: do philosophical positions drive one to despair, or do despairing feelings lead to bleak philosophical beliefs? One recalls Bradley's "confession" in the Preface to *Appearance and Reality*: "'Metaphysics is the finding of bad reasons for what we believe upon instinct.'" [26] Eliot echoes this inconoclastic sentiment when he writes that "Coleridge's metaphysical interest was quite genuine, and was, like most metaphysical interest, an affair of his emotions." [27] Whether one concludes that Eliot's philosophy determined or merely colored his emotional outlook, I believe that Bradley's philosophy had a positive effect on Eliot.

Both Eliot and Bradley believed that thought distorts experience by fragmenting its wholeness and that as a result we can never fully know "reality." Whiteside thinks that this attitude betrays a "distrust of thought," or what another critic calls Eliot's "fear of the intellect." [28] I would rather say it demonstrates an appreciation of the intellect's limits. Eliot went beyond Bradley in holding that the existence of the

25. Ibid., p. 404. See also Lyndall Gordon, *Eliot's Early Years* (New York: Oxford University Press, 1977), p. 53.

26. F. H. Bradley, *Appearance and Reality* (Oxford: Clarendon Press, 1969), p. xiv.

27. Eliot, "The Perfect Critic," in *The Sacred Wood* (1920; reprinted London: Methuen, 1960), p. 12.

28. Whiteside, "T. S. Eliot's Dissertation," p. 402; Richard Wollheim, "Eliot and F. H. Bradley: An Account," in *Eliot in Perspective,* ed. Graham Martin (New York: Humanities Press, 1970), p. 190.

Absolute could not even be inferred, much less directly known. Reason could therefore demarcate the place where faith, if necessary and if possible, must be called in. Eliot is extremely sensitive to the times when philosophers call faith to their rescue—whether it's a question of Bradley's Absolute or Bertrand Russell's conception of the "objects" studied by science. Eliot concludes that "a philosophy can and must be worked out with the greatest rigor and discipline in the details, but can ultimately be founded on nothing but faith." [29] Since the Absolute is founded on faith rather than reason, Eliot very properly says that "the ultimate nature of the Absolute is not within the scope of the present paper." He accepts "immediate experience" and the "Absolute" merely as the "hypothetical limits" of human perception. [30] It is in this context that he says that "immediate experience" is "annihilation and utter night." This statement betrays no despair. One could imagine Eliot despairing at an inability to believe that the Absolute unified experience only if he seemed to struggle with the notion. On the contrary, he dismisses it in the first chapter of his dissertation and contents himself with examining the "rigor and discipline in the details" of Bradley's philosophy. The "embrace [of] Bradleian monism," if one can call it that, was coldly formal.

An appreciation of Eliot's formal, critical interest in Bradley also indicates that he was not overcome by Bradley's alleged "solipsism." Concerning the famous *Waste Land* quotation "the whole world for each is peculiar and private to that soul," Whiteside says that "there is despair in [Eliot's] endorsement of Bradley's solipsistic statement"—not only in the notes but also in an essay on Bradley and Leibniz in 1916. [31] In the essay, however, which was written just after

29. Eliot, *Knowledge and Experience,* p. 163.
30. Ibid., p. 31.
31. Whiteside, "T. S. Eliot's Dissertation," p. 421.

the dissertation, he is far from endorsing Bradley. Eliot writes of the quotation, "Perhaps this is only a statement of a usual idealistic position, but never has it been put in a form so extreme." He notes that the extremity is a matter of emphasis and, in continuing his critical remarks on "usual idealistic positions," quotes the more "orthodox" position of Bernard Bosanquet: "a particular consciousness . . . is always and essentially a member of a further whole of experience." [32] Out of context, Bradley's statement does indeed enforce the somberness of Eliot's lines "I have heard the key / Turn in the door once and turn once only"; [33] but nothing indicates that Eliot considers Bradley's words to represent an authoritative statement of the fact of human isolation.

Eliot neither endorses nor, as F. R. Leavis writes, makes an "appeal" to Bradley's description of the isolated self. [34] Rather Eliot's reading of Bradley made him critical of any philosophical pretentions to tell the facts of human existence, including even Bradley's very mild pretentions. In the Conclusion to *Knowledge and Experience,* Eliot states that he is using an "empirical" method:

> demanding at the start what it is that we know for most certain (and this method deserves the name of empiricism as

32. Eliot, *Knowledge and Experience,* pp. 203, 204.

33. Eliot, "The Waste Land," in *Collected Poems, 1909-1962* (New York: Harcourt Brace Jovanovich, 1963), p. 69.

34. F. R. Leavis, *The Living Principle* (New York: Oxford University Press, 1975), p. 199. Leavis's hostile interpretation of what "reality" meant to Eliot ("the supremely Real is the completely Other") contrasts vividly with J. Hillis Miller's in *Poets of Reality* (New York: Atheneum, 1974), according to which Eliot eventually escapes Bradley's "subjective idealism" and accepts the "conditions of the real world." Richard Wollheim (in "Eliot and F. H. Bradley," p. 186) says that *The Waste Land*'s Bradley quotation illustrates "not Bradley's solipsism but rather his ambiguity or ambivalence on the subject of 'the common world.'" Wollheim therefore thinks that the Bradley passage is not really apposite to the poetry.

much as anything does) we find that we are certain of everything,—relatively, and of nothing,—positively, and that no knowledge will survive analysis. The virtue of metaphysical analysis is in showing the destructibility of everything, since analysis gives us something equally real, and for some purposes more real, than that which is analysed.

Nothing is more real than the play of the mind itself, which tells us that there is no such thing as philosophical certitude. He retains the skeptical elements of Bradley's system—in particular, the relativistic "degrees of truth" principle—and rejects the notion that we can know the "Absolute." As Hugh Kenner observes, Bradley gave Eliot a "deeply-thought-out *metaphysical* scepticism" and a "polemical strategy" for his future work.[35]

The beginnings of Eliot's "strategy" may be seen in the dissertation's references to Bertrand Russell, which I will return to, and in the statement that if one adheres "to a strictly common-sense view (which may be defined, I presume, as that which insists on the reality of the more primary objects) the theories of speculative physics seem perhaps as chimerical and uncalled-for as those of metaphysics."[36] This skepticism concerning the scientific version of "reality" is similar in tone to Wyndham Lewis's in *Time and Western Man.* Both writers attack the loose way "realism" and "idealism" is used in post-Bradeleian philosophy, and both are quick to detect mere rhetoric in philosophical thought.

Besides being generally influential (and notorious) in the twenties and thirties, *Time and Western Man* was a particular influence on Eliot, who read and discussed the book with

35. Hugh Kenner, *The Invisible Poet: T. S. Eliot* (New York: Ivan Obolensky, 1959), p. 47.
36. Eliot, *Knowledge and Experience,* p. 162.

Lewis while it was still in manuscript.[37] Although Eliot and Lewis were highly independent thinkers whose religious orientation and rhetorical techniques differed greatly, they converged upon a single position.

Time and Western Man is often considered a wild Quixote-like attack on the entire twentieth century. "Time" seems so sweeping a basis for an attack on the intellectual giants of the modern age, including Joyce, Bergson, and Whitehead, that only Lewis's bitter temper apparently accounts for his choice of victims. F. R. Leavis thought that a mere "list of names brought together under the 'Time-philosophy'" showed that Lewis couldn't think.[38] Indeed, Lewis is guilty of overreaching at times, and his attacks on the "philosophical ruffian" Bergson are excessive. Yet Lewis's attacks are no more sweeping than Eliot's on the "dissociation of sensibility" or Ezra Pound's on "abstraction." For Lewis, "Time" represents the spirit of abstraction that Eliot and Pound also attacked. The theme of Lewis's work is found in Eliot's "Whispers of Immortality," in which even philosophical entities are drawn to the fatal vulgarity of Grishkin (the "her" of the following lines):

> And even the Abstract Entities
> Circumambulate her charm;
> But our lot crawls between dry ribs
> To keep our metaphysics warm.[39]

37. In a letter to Eliot (February 1924), Lewis includes part of the *Time and Western Man* manuscript: ". . . I will send you a few more sections to cast a little more light on this. I want your opinion of it as a—what, a colleague." This letter and a later one conclude with plans for Eliot and Lewis to discuss the manuscript when they meet. See *The Letters of Wyndham Lewis,* ed. W. K. Rose (Norfolk, Conn.: New Directions, 1963), pp. 139–40.

38. F. R. Leavis, *The Common Pursuit* (London: Chatto & Windus, 1952), p. 243.

39. T. S. Eliot, *Collected Poems,* p. 46.

Lewis might be commenting on this passage when he attacks contemporary metaphysics and the scientific conception of the fundamental units of reality: "those very abstract entities . . . a thing-in-itself [or] the fundamental point-instant of space-time."[40] As many critics have observed, "Whispers of Immortality" comments on the "dissociation of sensibility" in modern thought that Eliot traced to the seventeenth century. The "Abstract Entities" symptomize the failure of "a direct sensuous apprehension of thought" in twentieth-century metaphysics.[41]

Lewis states the thesis of *Time and Western Man* when confuting the "realist" Alfred North Whitehead, whose reputation as a "critic of abstractions" and defender of the (romantic) poet's view of the world is for Lewis wholly misleading. Whitehead's reality is that of primary objects, such as color and form, which cannot be sensuously apprehended. In *Science and the Modern World,* Whitehead says that "the doctrine [of organic mechanism] which I am maintaining is that the whole concept of materialism only applies to very abstract entities, the products of logical discernment."[42] Lewis comments: "The only kind of thing that can be described as 'matter,' then, is such a thing as his 'eternal' entity colour. A colour is eternal. 'It haunts time like a spirit.' Is it not strange that the only sort of 'material' thing that Professor Whitehead will allow should remind him of a *spirit*? Yet it does; and that use of works is not without significance, nor a slip of a pen."[43]

This criticism of Whitehead leads Lewis to the "fundamen-

40. Lewis, *Time and Western Man,* p. 177.
41. Eliot, "The Metaphysical Poets," in *Selected Essays* (New York: Harcourt Brace Jovanovich, 1964), p. 426.
42. Alfred North Whitehead, *Science and the Modern World* (New York: New American Library, 1948), p. 76.
43. Lewis, *Time and Western Man,* p. 176.

tal issue" of his book: "the problem of the 'abstract' versus the 'concrete' at the base of the various world-pictures to be discussed. For what I have called the time-school, time and change are the ultimate reality. They are the *abstract school,* it could be said."[44] Time enters these "world-pictures" because the "objects" that the "realists" believe exist independently of the mind are conditioned by it. In *Our Knowledge of the External World,* Bertrand Russell reveals the way objects, for all their independent "reality," are dissolved in time: "A thing may be defined as a certain series of appearances. . . . Consider, say, a wall-paper which fades in the course of years. . . . the assumption that there is a constant entity, the wall-paper, which 'has' these various colours at various times, is a piece of gratuituous metaphysics."[45] From this point of view, "reality" is in time, not in the thing; or rather a space-time "event" replaces the thing. Russell's own term for the basic units of reality, "neutral entities," recalls Whitehead's "abstract entities." Lewis thus complains that the objects Russell holds "up to us, as our mirrors or as pictures of *our* reality, are of [a] mixed, fluid and neutral character" that dissociates them from sense experience.[46]

Eliot objects to Russell's entities for a more technical reason than Lewis. In his dissertation, Eliot notes that the difficulty with Russell's "neutral entities" is that they are neither real nor ideal, neither physical nor mental. The problem is "how we proceed from acquaintance with entities which are neither real nor unreal to a knowledge of real objects which is true or false."[47] Russell's neutral entities are, moreover, neither in time nor out of it, and to Eliot this is an

44. Ibid., p. 169.
45. Bertrand Russell, *Our Knowledge of the External World* (London: Allen & Unwin, 1922), pp. 111–12.
46. Lewis, *Time and Western Man,* p. 209.
47. Eliot, *Knowledge and Experience,* p. 108.

evasion rather than a solution of the "time difficulty in perception."[48] Eliot also treats this problem in the opening of "Burnt Norton," when (with perhaps Bergson more in mind than Russell) he writes of the way time past, present, and future prevent any steady perception of the world. Lewis dislikes Russell's "serial view of the object" because, to use Eliot's terms, it reduces experience to a "flicker / Over the strained time-ridden faces."[49] Eliot writes, "We cannot allow Mr. Russell's supposition of a 'consciousness' which might merely exist for a moment and experience a sensation of red."[50] Both Lewis and Eliot desire more permanence in the objects of perception: not a "flicker" but "daylight / Investing form with lucid stillness."[51] Eliot concludes that "any object which is wholly real is independent of time."[52]

To find a philosophy that asserts the concreteness of objects one must in fact turn to Idealism. The so-called Idealists give one a concrete, common-sense world and the so-called Realists (or "New" or "Critical" Realists) a sensuously dissociated world of space-time events. Lewis particularly admires Bradley and Bernard Bosanquet. The reason he admires Bosanquet is implicit in T. S. Eliot's reference to the "materialism, which (as exemplified particularly in the work of Mr. Bosanquet) from one point of view may very justly be said to lie at the basis of idealism."[53] And it was F. H. Bradley who wrote, in a passage especially admired by Eliot, that "'the sensuous curtain is a deception and a cheat, if it hides some colourless movement of atoms, some spectral

48. Ibid., p. 111.
49. "Burnt Norton," III, in *Collected Poems,* p. 178.
50. *Knowledge and Experience,* p. 29.
51. "Burnt Norton," III, in *Collected Poems,* p. 178.
52. *Knowledge and Experience,* p.110.
53. Ibid., p. 153.

woof of impalpable abstractions.'"[54] For Bradley, "reality is sentient experience . . . to be real is to be indissolubly one thing with sentience."[55]

Lewis is the first to admit the oddity of Idealism rather than "Realism" presenting a concrete, sensuous world. "But that is a paradox," Lewis warns, "that it is extremely important to lay hold of at the outset."[56] Moreover, this paradox is historically venerable, for one finds it in the work of Bishop Berkeley, who could never understand why his Idealism was taken as an affront to common sense. Berkeley took the extreme Idealist position—one from which Eliot was careful to dissociate Bradley—that the existence of objects is dependent on our perception of them. But extreme as his doctrine of objects seems, Lewis says that it was a valid attempt "to destroy the myth of the superiority of the 'abstract' over the immediate and individual."[57] For Bishop Berkeley, as for Bradley, there is no thing-in-itself or any neutral or abstract entity that accounts for appearances. Berkeley's things are what they appear to be. Lewis's admiration for Berkeley's "realism" anticipates later views of Berkeley's philosophy. Richard Popkin summarizes these views in an essay on Berkeley's "New Realism," which treats Berkeley "not as the upholder of some kind of philosophical daydream verging on madness, but rather as a hardheaded student of philosophy who sees that modern thought has

54. Eliot quotes this passage in his "F. H. Bradley," in *Selected Essays,* p. 397.

55. Bradley, *Appearance and Reality,* p. 128. For further comment on the "reality" of Bradley's appearances, see E. P. Bollier, "T. S. Eliot and F. H. Bradley: A Question of Influence," *Tulane Studies in English* 12 (1962):87–111.

56. Lewis, *Time and Western Man,* p. 169.

57. Ibid., p. 172.

culminated in a complete denial of the existence of the ordinary world." Popkin quotes a relevant passage from Berkeley's *Commentaries*: "Ask a man never tainted with [the philosophers's] jargon what he means by corporeal substance. . . . He shall answer Bulk, Solidity & such like sensible qualitys. These I retain."[58] In other words, he rejects the philosopher's "abstract entities" and says that the "sensible qualities" alone are real. Berkeley rejected what he considered, in Popkin's words, "a shadowy useless, physical reality, unbeknownst to us . . . lurking around somewhere."[59] Eliot rejected Russell's "dualistic realism" in similar terms: "A real (physical) world is assumed, then when we come to ask how we know this world, it appears that all we are sure of is certain data and forms of immediate experience, out of which the physical world is constructed—as a consequence of which the 'objectivity' of the external world becomes otiose or meaningless."[60]

Bishop Berkeley's stand against what he called "abstract ideas" explains why he was a hero to Lewis, as he was to W. B. Yeats. This link between Berkeley and Lewis also helps account for Yeats's admiration for Lewis. ("Tell Wyndham Lewis," Yeats wrote to a friend after reading *Time and Western Man*, "that I am in all essentials his most humble and admiring disciple.")[61] According to Yeats and Lewis, Bishop Berkeley's importance to modern thought was his emphasis on the mind as an active, creative force. Yeats writes that "only where the mind partakes of a pure activity

58. Richard H. Popkin, "The New Realism of Bishop Berkeley," in *George Berkeley,* ed. S. C. Pepper (Berkeley: University of California Press, 1957), p. 9.

59. Ibid., p. 5.

60. Eliot, *Knowledge and Experience,* p. 111.

61. Yeats, *The Letters of W. B. Yeats,* ed. Allen Wade (London: Rupert Hart-Davis, 1954), pp. 733–34.

can art or life attain swiftness, volume, unity," and it attains these things in Berkeley's philosophy.[62] For this reason, Berkeley will be the inspiration for Lewis's attempt to state a philosophical position to replace the "abstract school."

In his essay on Irving Babbitt, Eliot notes that it is easier to destroy theories one dislikes than to build a "constructive philosophy": "Mr. Wyndham Lewis is obviously striving courageously toward a positive theory, but in his published work has not yet reached that point."[63] The conclusion to *Time and Western Man* promises to publish "the particular beliefs that are explicit" in its criticisms. Although this work never appeared, one can speculate that Lewis was attempting to go far beyond his depth and state a theory of the creativity of the mind for the twentieth century as Berkeley (after all, unsuccessfully) did for the eighteenth century.

All that survives of Lewis's intention is a non-Romantic interpretation of the mind's creativity. It is "non-Romantic" because Lewis, unlike Ezra Pound, asserts no congruity between the forces of the human mind and those of the universe. The artist is—to use the title of Lewis's 1914 drama—an "enemy of the stars," who defies the powers of nature or life. By "life" Lewis means the merely emotional life, or the life given over passively to the flux of phenomena. The artist must stop time. In Lewis's wonderfully still self-portrait (Fig. 16) the artist's easel slashes through the blank clock face in the background. The artist's mind must order the flow of time, and this order alone constitutes "reality." At times Lewis seems to identify reality with the mind's understanding of it. Eliot explains the relation of the mind's order to reality more carefully than Lewis when he writes that the function of art lies "in imposing a credible order

62. Yeats, *Essays and Introductions,* p. 405.
63. Eliot, "The Humanism of Irving Babbitt," in *Selected Essays,* p. 419.

16. Wyndham Lewis, *Portrait of the Artist*. City Art Gallery, Manchester.

upon ordinary reality, and thereby eliciting some perception of an order *in* reality." [64]

In *Time and Western Man,* Lewis illustrates his theory of the mind by raising the standard philosophical illustration of the reality of a penny, which may, depending on one's angle of vision, appear round or oblong. "There is the *scientific penny,* the *perceptual penny,* the *optical penny*. . . . The penny of common sense is, however, a very sophisticated affair indeed compared with the optical penny." [65] It is "sophisticated" because the common-sense penny is a composite of the scientific penny (a mass of particles), the perceptual penny (the sensum that causes us to perceive the coin in a certain way), and the optical penny (what we in fact see in a certain configuration). The scientific object or "event" is a function of time as well as of space; however, our minds can triumph over the dissolving power of time. When we look at a penny we apprehend it as if we saw all around it—as if we were in several places at the same time— and also as if we were touching it. Lewis sometimes refers to his work as the "philosophy of the eye," but he warns that we must not dissociate the sense of sight from our other senses. In Lewis's *Childermass,* for example, the character of the Bailiff represents the distortions of the ear and Hyperides those of the eye. Since neither sense alone is capable of true perception, both characters are deluded. For Lewis, it is the scientist who is the victim of what Coleridge called the "despotism of the eye." He uses his analysis of the way we perceive objects to show that our minds are never passive recipients of experience: "'Objects' are the finished products

64. Eliot, "Poetry and Drama," in *On Poetry and Poets* (New York: Farrar, Straus & Giroux, 1961), p. 94. Careful as this formulation is, it might well have seemed imprecise to Eliot in 1916.
65. Lewis, *Time and Western Man,* p. 416.

of our perceptive faculty, they are the result . . . of the organizing activity of our minds. When we say we *see* them, in reality what we perceive is not the direct datum of sensation, but an elaborate and sophisticated entity, or 'object.' We do even in that sense 'create' them more than 'see' them."[66]

Eliot could not have approved of Lewis's use of "create" in this context, although presumably Pound would have welcomed it. When Eliot speaks of the world "as constructed, or constructing itself," he says that he is "careful not to talk of the creative activity of mind, a phrase meaningless in metaphysics."[67] Nevertheless, Bradley's philosophy provides him with a theory of language that does imply, for the poet at least, a "creative activity of mind." In his dissertation, Eliot denies that the "ideas of a great poet are in any sense arbitrary. . . . In really great imaginative work the connections are felt to be bound by as logical necessity as any connections to be found anywhere."[68] The poet's status is further raised by the interdependence of reality and our molding of it through language. With an echo of "Prufrock," Eliot denies that there is an external world "laid out upon a table" for our objective examination; reality is "in a sense dependent upon thought."[69] (In a canceled line of *The Waste Land,* he says that London lives only "in the awareness of the observing eye.")[70] Eliot thinks of "the world not as ready made—the world, that is, of meaning for us—but as constructed, or constructing itself . . . at every moment."[71] Lan-

66. Ibid., p. 373.
67. Eliot, *Knowledge and Experience,* p. 136.
68. Ibid., p. 75.
69. Ibid., p. 57.
70. Eliot, *The Waste Land: A Facsimile,* ed. Valerie Eliot (New York: Harcourt Brace Jovanovich, 1971), p. 43.
71. Eliot, *Knowledge and Experience,* p. 136.

guage is integral to this process of construction: "It is not true that language is simply a development of our ideas; it is a development of reality as well. The idea is developed from within, as language shows a richness of content and intricacy of connections which it assumes to have been really there, but which are as well an enrichment of the reality grasped."[72] Although there is no suggestion here of romantic "creativity," or of language as creating the forms of thought, this passage could indicate, as in Lewis's theories, that the artist makes a uniquely important contribution to the shaping of reality.

Any individual may either passively accede to experience or use the organizing power of his mind to the full. Reality thus depends on the ability of the self to integrate its experience. Eliot speaks of the "life of a soul" as engaging in the "painful task of unifying . . . jarring and incompatible" worlds of experience.[73] Lewis's conception of the self is similar, and as the following passage shows, is similarly influenced by Bradley:

> In Bradley's account of the degrees of reality the amount that an individual possesses can be tested by the amount of strain beneath which he is able to retain the individuality, or the point at which that breaks down. The Absolute would be the individual of individuals, the self that has never broken down but has maintained its isolation. So according to that view, and according to ours, reality is to be sought in the self or the person.[74]

Although Lewis is critical of Bradley's Absolute, on the grounds that it makes the individual relatively insignificant,

72. Ibid., p. 44.
73. Ibid., p. 147.
74. Lewis, *Time and Western Man*, p. 471.

he approves of its transcendence. He dislikes the picture of an evolving or emerging God in Bergson and Whitehead because it substitutes flux for permanence even for the Deity. Quoting Bosanquet, Lewis says the issue is "'between time in the Absolute and the Absolute in time.'"[75] Lewis objects to what he calls this "eternal manufacturing of a God," which strikes him as the product of a mechanistic, industrial age. He notes that the word *dynamic* is used indiscriminately to describe "Big Business, . . . Wall Street, and Mussolini" as well as what one philosopher called Bergson's "'dynamic aspect of reality.'"[76] In a review he wrote for Lewis's magazine *The Enemy,* Eliot also linked Whitehead to the modern industrial ethos when he slyly suggested that Whitehead had stayed too long in America and now could value only a religion "on the make" or "in the making."[77]

For all his attempt to make a "positive statement," Lewis's review of contemporary science and philosophy makes him as skeptical as Eliot's dissertation helped to make him. The Conclusion of *Time and Western Man* returns to Bishop Berkeley for its inspiration, and delights in the paradox that Idealism provides a more sensuous, common-sense, "real" world than scientific and philosophical "Realism":

> It is argued here that the entire physical world is strictly unreal; and the unrealist part of it we believe is that part or

75. Ibid., p. 226.
76. Lewis, *Time and Western Man* (New York: Harcourt Brace, 1928; reprinted Boston: Beacon Press, 1957), p. xiii. Lewis added a new preface to the American edition.
77. Eliot, "The Return of Foxy Grandpa" (review of Alfred North Whitehead's *Science in the Modern World* and *Religion in the Making*), Wyndham Lewis Collection, Olin Library, Cornell University. In an undated letter in the Cornell Collection, Eliot asks Lewis if he would like a review of Whitehead from a point of view not identical to Lewis's but tending the same way. This review was set in type but never used— perhaps because of *The Enemy*'s brief, three-issue existence.

aspect supplied us by science. So with bridle and bit we ride the phantoms of sense, as though to the manner born. Or rather it would be more descriptive of our actual experience to say that, camped somnolently, in a relative repose of a god-like sort, upon the surface of this nihilism, we regard ourselves as at rest, with our droves of objects—trees, houses, hills— grouped round us.[78]

The term *god-like* is used with due irony. Although we can only "regard" ourselves as at rest and can no more than shepherd our "droves" of objects, still we have in some sense created our world. Like the world of Bishop Berkeley, one of the first to oppose the "dissociation of sensibility," Lewis's will have "Bulk, Solidity, & such like sensible quality."

Yeats complained that the Lockean abstractions had become the "ground-work of every text-book." Pound countered such generalities with the "luminous details" of his cantos. *Time and Western Man* was designed to clarify the philosophical and scientific assumptions that produced this oppressive climate of received opinions. Lewis felt that "everyday life is too much affected by the speculative activities that are renewing and transvaluing our world, for it to be able to survive in ignorance of those speculations."[79] Eliot combatted this ignorance through the *Criterion,* and thus shared with Lewis the hope for "a new learned minority . . . familiar enough with the abstract to be able to handle the concrete."[80] In the opening essay of *The Sacred Wood,* Eliot compared the "abstract style" of contemporary literary criticism with the "verbalism" that has characterized "the greater part of the philosophical output of the last hundred years." He dryly notes that "if verbalism were confined to

78. Lewis, *Time and Western Man* (British ed.), p. 473.
79. Ibid. (American ed.), p. vii.
80. Ibid., p. xii.

professional philosophers, no harm would be done. But their corruption has extended very far."[81] The only remedy is for the artist to oppose abstraction not only through the example of his art but also through direct criticism.

If Pound, Eliot, and Lewis converged upon a single attitude toward modern philosophy, it might be summed up in Pound's phrase "Go in fear of abstractions."[82] Their battle against the philosophical tendencies of their age reveals them in their roles as "dispossessed artists," to use Eliot's definitive phrase, who are "driven to examining the elements in the situation—political, social, philosophical, or religious—which frustrate [their] labour."[83] The following chapter will examine this dispossession in the political rather than the philosophical world, where the consequences were more troubling.

81. "The Perfect Critic," pp. 8–9.
82. Pound, *Literary Essays,* p. 5.
83. Eliot, "Commentary," *Criterion* 4 (June 1926):424. Eliot is commenting on Lewis's *Art of Being Ruled* (1926), which preceded *Time and Western Man* by a year.

6

James Joyce and the
Vortex of History

> We see two hostile ideologies contending for the mastery of
> the world—Communism and Fascism. Both advance their
> policies (they cannot do otherwise) in a paralysing atmosphere
> of martial law. And the constraints, the pseudo-religious inten-
> sity, of these systems, do not lend themselves to the relaxations
> of the senses, nor to the detached delights of the intellect, what-
> ever else may be claimed for them.
>
> —Wyndham Lewis, *Blasting and Bombardiering*

The Vortex was never powerful enough to draw James
Joyce within its field. The pattern for his relationship with
Pound, Eliot, and Lewis was set when Pound tried to include
Joyce's work in *Blast.* Thanks to its "metallic exactitude"
(Pound's phrase), Joyce's prose would have fitted into the
Vorticist journal like a cartridge into a pistol (for *Blast's*
mission was to "kill John Bull with art.") As the editor of
Blast, however, Lewis would not admit Joyce into his rebel
band. Pound wrote to Joyce in 1914 that Lewis "likes the
novel [*A Portrait of the Artist*] but isn't very keen on the
stories."[1] Joyce's *Portrait* was then being serialized in *The*

---

1. Forrest Read, ed., *Pound/Joyce: Letters and Essays* (New York:
New Directions, 1967), p. 26. In *Blasting and Bombardiering* (London:
Eyre & Spottiswoode, 1937), Lewis recalls that "*Some* pages of the
'Portrait' I had read, when it first appeared as a serial in the *Egoist*. . . .
But I took very little interest. At that time, it was of far too tenuous an
elegance for my taste. Its flavour was altogether too literary. And as to
its emotional content, that I condemned at once as sentimental Irish" (p.
271).

Egoist, where it was soon followed by the serialization of Lewis's first novel, *Tarr.* Joyce's novel could not appear in both *The Egoist* and *Blast,* which may account for Lewis's claim that he liked the novel rather than the stories. Judging from his later criticism, Lewis in fact always disliked both *A Portrait* and *Dubliners* for what he considered its *passéiste* and provincial tone. Whereas the Vorticist kept his wide-awake eye on the present, Lewis felt that Joyce cocked his ear exclusively toward the past.

Pound championed Lewis and Joyce on equal terms when he wrote in 1920 that "the English prose fiction of my decade is the work of this pair of authors."[2] Such comparisons, as well as the serializations of both of their first novels in *The Egoist,* established their lifelong rivalry. Although Lewis's objections to Joyce's art were always sincere, this rivalry or competition helps to explain Lewis's reluctance to have Joyce's work appear in *Blast.* Lewis's motives were certainly personal when he offered and then refused to publish Joyce's work during the 1920s. In May 1926 Joyce wrote to Harriet Shaw Weaver that Lewis was beginning a critical review that would, as an exception to its rule of excluding creative work, publish a section of "Work in Progress," as the early drafts of *Finnegans Wake* were called. By September 1926 Joyce was expecting Lewis to publish "The Four Watches of Shem," which Sylvia Beach had sent to Lewis for the first issue of his review. When Lewis's new periodical appeared, however, bearing the unexpected and ominous title *The Enemy,* it contained only Lewis's attack on Joyce as a writer who was contributing to literary and social decadence. Lewis's essay "The Revolutionary Simpleton," which takes up some 90 percent of the first issue of *The Enemy,* uses

2. Pound, *The Literary Essays of Ezra Pound,* ed. T. S. Eliot (New York: New Directions, 1968), p. 424.

Ezra Pound and Gertrude Stein as well as Joyce to show how modern writers uncritically echo "revolutionary" ideas in their art. As a radical turned traditionalist, Lewis intended to unmask the social nihilism behind avant-garde art.

In a section of *The Enemy* entitled "An Analysis of the Mind of James Joyce," Lewis writes that "the work of Mr. Joyce enters in various ways as a specimen into the critical scheme I am outlining."[3] One suspects that Lewis was always and only interested in Joyce's work as a "specimen," which may explain why he would have made an "exception" in order to publish "Work in Progress" in his critical review. Although Lewis's analysis of Joyce in *The Enemy* concentrates on *Ulysses,* he does cite a passage from Joyce's later work that had appeared in *This Quarter* to show that Joyce's concern (in this case, whether Shem the penman is a gentleman) "is strangely of another day, or, on the prinicple of the time-philosophy, provincial."[4] Thus Lewis fulfilled the letter, if scarcely the spirit, of his promise to publish a section of "Work in Progress."

Although Lewis did not treat Joyce fairly, his editorial treatment of "Work in Progress" was no worse than Joyce had come to expect. Printer's errors and publication delays made Joyce's experiences with the *transatlantic review, This Quarter,* and *The Calendar of Modern Letters* uniformly distressing. T. S. Eliot published a section of Joyce's new work in *The Criterion* in 1925, but asked for no further contributions; and in 1928 Joyce was dismayed when Eliot's quarterly published Sean O'Faolain's criticism of "Work in Progress." With a thesis Lewis would have approved, O'Fao-

3. Wyndham Lewis, *The Enemy: A Review of Art and Literature,* no. 1 (January 1927), p. 95.
4. Ibid., p. 126; Lewis refers to Joyce's episode "Shem the Penman," which appeared in *This Quarter* (Autumn–Winter, 1925–26).

lain attacked the work on the grounds that Joyce was trying to personalize language when by its nature it must be impersonal and traditional.[5]

After the first series of Pound's providential interventions in Joyce's career, culminating in the arrangement to have Harriet Shaw Weaver subsidize Joyce's work, his dealings with Joyce were no more satisfactory than Eliot's or Lewis's. Pound was at first enthusiastic about "Work in Progress" and told Joyce in 1923 that the first pages of the *transatlantic review* were to be reserved for him "with a trumpet blast."[6] Since he had no word from Lewis about publishing a section of his new work, Joyce was pleased to send Pound the "Four Watches of Shem" in November 1926 for Pound's new journal *The Exile.* After a quick reading, Pound replied that he could make nothing of the excerpt and doubted the value of its intricate style: "Nothing short of divine vision or a new cure for the clapp can possibly be worth all the circumambient peripherization."[7]

Although Joyce's Vorticist friends were fainthearted and shortsighted about the value of "Work in Progress," one cannot question the honesty of their judgments. Even Lewis presented what Joyce himself respected as the best hostile criticism of *Ulysses.*[8] Moreover, Joyce appreciated the publicity value of serving as the "Enemy's" target and was eager to debate the issues Lewis raised. *The Enemy* had at least paid Joyce the compliment of well-argued attacks on *Ulysses*

5. Sean O'Faolain, "Style and the Limitations of Speech," *Criterion* 8 (September 1928):67–87.

6. Joyce, *The Letters of James Joyce,* 3 vols. (New York: Viking Press, 1957), vol. 1, ed. Stuart Gilbert, p. 204.

7. Pound, *Selected Letters of Ezra Pound, 1907–1941,* ed. D. D. Paige (New York: New Directions, 1971), p. 202. Joyce replied to Pound's comment by making one of the titles of ALP's "mamafesta" "A New Cure for an Old Clap" (*Finnegans Wake* [New York: Viking Press, 1962], p. 104).

8. Joyce, *Letters,* vol. 3, ed. Richard Ellmann, p. 250.

and "Work in Progress." To return the compliment, Joyce drew Lewis into the vortex of *Finnegans Wake,* where the forces of Joyce's artistic universe warped and transformed Lewis's terms.

In the early twenties, Joyce and Lewis were friends as well as rivals. Lewis recorded his first meeting with the man he called the "Dante of Dublin" in his autobiography *Blasting and Bombardiering* (1937). Together with T. S. Eliot, Lewis delivered in 1920 (as if he were Joyce's own Shaun the Post) a brown-paper parcel on behalf of Ezra Pound. When Joyce finally undid "the crafty housewifely knots of the cunning old Ezra," the three writers discovered, "along with some nondescript garments for the trunk . . . a fairly presentable pair of *old brown shoes.*"[9] Joyce never recovered from receiving this embarrassing charity from "the good-hearted American," as Lewis called Pound, and thereafter always insisted on paying for the lavish entertainment of his new friends. Although Joyce never became friendly with Eliot, he liked Lewis and his works, such as *Tarr,* the play *The Ideal Giant,* and the short story "Cantleman's Spring-Mate," which provoked the suppression of one issue of *The Little Review.* ("You will enjoy cattlemen's spring meat," Joyce writes in the *Wake.*) Joyce was usually guarded about his personal friendships, but he wrote enthusiastically to Frank Budgen that he had "several uproarious allnight sittings (and dancings) with Lewis as he will perhaps tell you. I like him."[10] During Lewis's frequent visits to Paris in the twenties, they became drinking as well as literary rivals. Ezra Pound recalled that they would try to "out do each other drinking. One night they about killed each other."[11] Joyce

9. Lewis, *Blasting and Bombardiering,* pp. 274–75.
10. Joyce, *Letters,* 3:42.
11. Quoted in *Charles Olson and Ezra Pound: An Encounter at St. Elizabeths,* ed. Catherine Seeley (New York: Viking Press, 1975), p. 107.

alludes to this incident, or perhaps another like it, in his fable of the Ondt (in this context representing Lewis) and the Gracehoper (Joyce), when the Gracehoper's indulgence leaves him "as sieck as a sexton and tantoo pooveroo quant a churchprince."[12] Despite the Ondt's pose, like Lewis's own, as a "confirmed aceticist and aristoaller," the Ondt is just as debauched as the Gracehoper and cavorts with the same "houris" as his rival: "Never did Dorsan from Dunshanagan dance it with more devilry!"[13] (According to Richard Ellmann, it was Joyce who once kept Lewis from a "lapse of decorum" with a prostitute by reminding him that he was the author of *The Ideal Giant*.)[14] Lewis also fell "sieck" after what he recalls as three straight nights of revelry and could not be awakened for a full day afterward: "All this was bad for Joyce's rheumatic eyes," Lewis remembered, "and Mrs. Joyce objected to my presence in Paris then."[15]

Lewis later reconciled himself with Mrs. Joyce; it was Joyce himself he fell out with as their artistic paths continued to diverge. Their aesthetic differences were evident from the first days of their friendship, when they visited Rouen Cathedral and Lewis criticized its Gothic facade: "the spatial intemperance, the nervous multiplication of detail. Joyce listened and then remarked that he . . . himself, as a matter of fact, in words, did something of that sort."[16] Lewis created a visual equivalent of this "nervous multiplication of detail" in his wonderfully intricate sketch of Joyce as the "Duc de Joyeux" (Fig. 12), in which the sketch is saved from "spatial intemperance" by what Walter Michel calls the strict

12. Joyce, *Finnegans Wake*, p. 416.
13. Ibid., p. 417.
14. Richard Ellmann, *James Joyce* (New York: Oxford University Press, 1959), p. 530.
15. Lewis, *Blasting and Bombardiering*, p. 238.
16. Wyndham Lewis, *Rude Assignment: A Narrative of My Career Up-to-Date* (London: Hutchinson, 1950), p. 56.

"totem-pole structure" of the design.[17] Although Lewis saw
the difference between them as that of a classic versus a
romantic sensibility, the terms he emphasized, and the ones
Joyce accepted, employed the words *time* and *space*. In *The
Enemy,* Lewis writes that "I regard *Ulysses* as a *time-book*;
and by that I mean that it lays emphasis upon . . . the self-
conscious time-sense, that has now been erected into a
universal philosophy."[18] According to this Bergsonian "philosophy," all experience is in a condition of becoming rather
than in a state of being. A classical sense of form and
stability is thus swamped with a romantic feeling for dynamic activity. Although Lewis sincerely, even warmly,
admired the "physical enthusiasm" of Joyce's realism, he
thought that one is soon glutted with the details of June 16,
1904, in *Ulysses*: "the dates of the various toothpastes, the
brewery and laundry receipts, the growing pile of punched
'bus-tickets'" produced "by the obsessional application of
the naturalistic method associated with the exacerbated time-
sense." Lewis concludes that this "torrent of matter is the
einsteinian flux [or] the duration-flux of Bergson."[19]

Lewis understood that Joyce intended to transcend time
and reach the aesthetic condition of freedom from space and
time limits. But he denied that Joyce's art achieves this
condition: "The method of *Ulysses* imposes a softness,
flabbiness and vagueness everywhere in its bergsonian fluid-
ity."[20] Lewis was not merely challenging Joyce on theoretical
or critical grounds. He was brave enough to publish works

17. Walter Michel, *Wyndham Lewis: Paintings and Drawings* (Berkeley
and Los Angeles: University of California Press), p. 111.
18. Lewis, "The Revolutionary Simpleton," *The Enemy,* no. 1 (January
1927), p. 103.
19. Wyndham Lewis, *Time and Western Man* (London: Chatto &
Windus, 1927), pp. 108, 119. Lewis reprints "An Analysis of the Mind of
James Joyce" from *The Enemy* in *Time and Western Man.*
20. Ibid., p. 120.

that allow his readers to see how his theoretical principles look in action. With the literary scene floodlit by his own critical prose, he published *The Childermass* (1928) and *The Apes of God* (1930), works whose "spatial" art would rival the achievement of the "time-book" *Ulysses*.[21]

Lewis was pleased when reviewers of *The Apes of God* used Remy de Gourmont's word *visuel* to describe him and called him a "personal appearance" satirist.[22] His long, brilliant descriptions—usually satiric portraits of the "apes" of the godlike artist—are stunning, slow-motion attacks that grind his victims out of existence, with the unfortunately ironic effect that his characters cannot interest the reader for more than a few pages. For example, his character Julius Ratner, an "ape" who fancies himself a "high-brow" writer, is described in pages of minute physical details interspersed with little or no narrative action. Here is Ratner washing his face:

> He slid his hands into the water. He soaped the channel between the muscles of the back of the neck, a hand limply hooked, with a row of four fingertips. The head moved upon its atlas, rubbing itself cat-like against the almost stationary fingers. Travelling forward over the occipital bones pimples were encountered. Working the antagonistic muscles framing the thyroid shields, he gently and limply rocked his head-piece.[23]

Although Geoffrey Wagner identifies Ratner as James Joyce, this particular ape, who indeed does write epiphanies

21. Joyce was amused to notice this rivalry; he wrote to Harriet Weaver: "Chatto and Windus put out a prospectus which Miss Beach has announcing a colossal new work in the press by Lewis. The text says 'the only work that can at all hold a card to it is ———.' You can supply the blank" (*Letters,* 3:173). Lewis's work was *The Childermass.*

22. See Wyndham Lewis, *Men without Art* (London: Cassell, 1934), pp. 118–19.

23. Wyndham Lewis, *The Apes of God* (1930; reprinted Baltimore: Penguin Books, 1965), p. 164.

("A little child picked a forget-me-not. She lifted a chalice. It was there. *Epiphany*."), is rather the ape of a real artist such as Joyce.[24] Lewis never doubted Joyce's greatness any more than he did Picasso's; it was the greatness of both men, he thought, that made their radical techniques dangerous for other artists. The character of James Pullman in *The Childermass,* on the other hand, is intended as a portrait of Joyce. The opening description of Pullman illustrates Lewis's sharp-focus style:

> At the ferry-station there is a frail figure planted on the discoloured stones facing the stream. Hatless, feet thrust into old leather slippers, the brown vamp prolonged up the instep by a japanned tongue of black, it might be a morning in the breezy popular summer, a visitor halted on the quay of the holiday-port, to watch the early-morning catch. Sandy-grey hair in dejected spandrils strays in rusty wisps: a thin rank moustache is pressed by the wind, bearing first from one direction then another, back against the small self-possessed mouth. Shoulders high and studious, the right arm hugs, as a paradoxical ally, a humble limb of nature, an oaken sapling Wicklow-bred. The suit of nondescript dark grey for ordinary day-wear, well-cut and a little shabby, is coquettishly tight and small, on the trunk and limbs of a child. Reaching up with a girlish hand to the stick cuddled under the miniature oxter, with the other hand the glasses are shaded against the light.[25]

Even a fine, full-length portrait such as this fails to fit into the narrative rhythm of the book. In defense of Lewis one might observe that he intends to break the narrative rhythm and to stop time through his descriptions. In the conclusion to his "Analysis of the Mind of James Joyce," he admits that

24. Geoffrey Wagner, *Wyndham Lewis: A Portrait of the Artist as the Enemy* (New Haven: Yale University Press, 1957), pp. 170–71; Lewis, *Apes of God,* p. 166.
25. Wyndham Lewis, *The Childermass* (London: Chatto & Windus, 1928), p. 2.

"it is a good deal as a pictorial and graphic artist that I approach these problems."[26] This approach produces novels in which an omniscient narrator is firmly in control of plot and characters. Lewis did not choose conventional narrative techniques for conventional reasons. His obsession was with controlling time, defining images, and expressing clear and distinct ideas, leads to such works as *Tarr, The Revenge for Love,* and *Self Condemned,* in which routine techniques are used with passionate conviction.

Nevertheless, his prose does not produce the aesthetic state he described so memorably when discussing the effect of paintings by Van Gogh, Rembrandt, and Picasso (the latter's portrait of Gertrude Stein): "'The course of time stops.' A sort of immortality descends upon these objects. It is an immortality which, in the case of the painting, they have to pay for with death, or at least with its coldness and immobility."[27] An allusion to this passage, or to one of the many others in which Lewis states the same idea, explains why Joyce's Professor Jones in *Finnegans Wake* says (p. 164) that only an "unskilled singer" would be guilty of "subordinating the space-element . . . to the time factor, which ought to be killed." In the debate of the Gracehoper and the Ondt, the Gracehoper has the last word on the time-space debate when he sings to the Ondt:

> Your genus its worldwide, your spacest sublime!
> But, Holy Saltmartin, why can't you beat time?"[28]

26. *The Enemy,* no. 1 (January 1927), p. 112.

27. Lewis, *Wyndham Lewis on Art,* ed. Walter Michel and C. J. Fox (New York: Funk & Wagnalls, 1969), p. 208. The quotation in this passage is from Arthur Schopenhauer.

28. Joyce, *Finnegans Wake,* p. 419. In *Our Friend James Joyce* (New York: Doubleday, 1958), Mary and Padraic Colum observe that Joyce is echoing Oliver Goldsmith's poem "Retaliation" in this couplet: "So Joyce had written the verse and the episode in which the verse occurs as a retaliation" (p. 147).

As the Gracehoper implies, Lewis's efforts to stop time merely destroy the narrative rhythm of fiction, which in its very nature is bound to time.

Joyce once remarked to Frank Budgen, "Allowing that the whole of what Lewis says about [*Ulysses*] is true, is it more than ten per cent of the truth?"[29] As I see it, Joyce's intricate reply to Lewis in *Finnegans Wake* is that Lewis has presented exactly 50 percent of the truth. His criticism of Joyce as a representative of the "time-mind" is a half-truth which at the very least needs the complementary admission that Lewis has an equally flawed space-mind. Joyce's strategy is to reveal Lewis's limitation through an analysis of the mind of Wyndham Lewis, which will in turn produce some half-truths about the space-mind. The resulting distortions will then have to be reconciled. The warring forces in *Finnegans Wake* are personified through Shem and Shaun, the twin sons of the *Wake*'s major figure, HCE. As Lewis's divisiveness is exposed, he becomes an avatar of Shaun. But Shaun stands for more than Lewis alone. Joyce's reply to Lewis's criticism is just as applicable to Pound's or Eliot's.

Although Joyce refers to Lewis throughout the *Wake,* we have noted that the "Ondt and the Gracehoper" section specifically answers the criticism first published in *The Enemy.* Two further sections of *Finnegans Wake,* linked by the hectoring comments of Professor Jones, are also important replies to Lewis: the fable of "The Mookse and the Gripes" and the story of Burrus and Caseous.

The lecture style of Joyce's Professor Jones is inspired largely by Lewis's style in *The Enemy.* In their reply to Lewis's "Enemy" incursions, the editors of *transition,* as publishers of Joyce's "Work in Progress," said that Lewis's

29. Frank Budgen, "Further Recollections of James Joyce," *Partisan Review* 23 (1956):539.

argument "slips from sight in digression, it is retrieved, patted and padded a bit, lost again, eventually recaught and pondered over until it falls apart into trivialities before the readers's weary eyes."[30] Joyce made this identification of Jones's style with Lewis's explicit when he told Harriet Shaw Weaver that Jones in "his know-all profoundly impressive role" was one "for which an 'ever devoted friend' (so [Lewis's] letters are signed) unrequestedly consented to pose."[31]

Professor Jones introduces the "dime-cash" (time is money) problem into the *Wake* "from the blinkpoint of so eminent a spatialist"—namely, himself. The context here is Question 11 of the "Questions" chapter in which Shem the Penman asks his brother Shaun if he would help him when in need. The combined character of Shaun-Jones violently replies, "No, blank ye," and lurches into a complicated argument, replete with learned references to "Bitchson," "Winestain," and "a recent postvortex piece infustigation" in order to justify his jealous contempt for his brother. As Jones has little faith in the intelligence of his "muddlecrass" audience, he uses a fable to illustrate his postvortex theory. In the ensuing fable of the Mookse and the Gripes, the Mookse (part monkey, in reference to Lewis's apes) stands for Lewis and the Gripes for Joyce—or, rather, for Joyce if he were as intolerant as Wyndham Lewis.[32]

Since the fable illustrates Lewis's intemperate abuse of any artistic credo different from his own, the Mookse is associated with the Catholic church at its most authoritarian. As

30. Eugene Jolas, Elliot Paul, and Robert Sage, "First Aid to the Enemy," *transition,* no. 9 (December 1927), p. 164.

31. Joyce, *Letters,* 1:257–58.

32. My account of Lewis's feud draws upon Dougald McMillan, *transition: The History of a Literary Era, 1927–1938* (New York: George Braziller, 1976), chaps. 13 and 14.

Padraic Colum recalls, Joyce delighted in imagining Lewis as a convert to Catholicism.[33] Thus the Mookse, having "vactincanated" his ears (against the siren song of "Work in Progress"), and with his "athemyst-sprinkled pederect" and his "unfallable encyclicling," encounters a "boggylooking stream"—the river Liffey, which runs through Dublin and is a major character (HCE's wife, Anna Livia Plurabelle) of the *Wake*. When the Gripes dares to address this visitor, the Mookse explodes in a combination of Lewis's language in *Blast* and that of the church: "Blast yourself and your anathmoy infairioriboos!" Undiscouraged, the Gripes mildly asks him for the time of day, and the Mookse's violent reaction reveals his Lewisian *idée fixe* about time: "Is this space of our couple of hours too dimensional for you, temporiser?" As the Gripes becomes infected with the Mookse's rancor, they argue so bitterly that they fail to notice Nuvoletta, a character who represents the feminine principle that could reconcile their warring contraries of space and time: "She tried to make the Mookse look up at her (but *he* was fore too adiaptotously farseeing) and to make the Gripes hear how coy she could be (though he was much to schystimatically auricular about *his ens* to heed her)." The Mookse's eye, which perceives things separated in space, does not truly see; nor does the Gripes's ear, which perceives experience in a time sequence, truly hear. Joyce implies that a reconciliation of these time and space principles should be possible, and in the Burrus and Caseous narrative that follows, he shows that it is the Lewis figure alone that prevents the reconciliation.

Immediately before the story of Burrus and Caseous, Professor Jones intervenes to congratulate himself on the

33. Mary and Padraic Colum, *Our Friend James Joyce*, p. 145.

effect of the Mookse and Gripes fable, concluding that it shows that he (Shaun-Lewis-Jones) is "a mouth's more deserving case by genius." As Jones vows his "symbathos for my ever devoted friend," the scene reveals Lewis vaunting himself and his "classical" art over Joyce and his temporal art. Lewis once told Joyce, presumably in jest, that he should emigrate to South America,[34] and Shaun-Jones expresses a similarly jealous wish about Shem: "I want him to go and live like a theabild in charge of the night brigade on Tristan da Cunha, isle of manoverboard." After this revelation of the petty motives behind his argument, Jones returns to the "space question where ever michelangelines have fooled to dread," which soon grows so complicated and allusive (in the style of *Time and Western Man*) that he loses control of his own argument and ultimately undercuts his own position.

Fearing that he has again lost his audience, Professor Jones tells a tale in which Burrus and Caseous replace the Mookse and the Gripes as the warring contraries of space and time. The Shem figure Caseous is described as a "puir tyron" because Lewis's art journal *The Tyro* attacked the "tyros" or amateurs of the art world. Burrus, on the other hand, is "a genuine prime, the real choice, full of natural greace." Jones can imagine no reconciliation between the two because "Caseous is obversely the revise of [Burrus]." Yet Jones becomes so entangled in his argument that he must warn his audience that "I am not out now to be taken up as unintentionally recommending the . . . helixtrolysis of these amboadipates." Nor should his argument be construed, he claims, as a "final endorsement" of two of Joyce's favorite philosophers, Nicholas of Cusa and Bruno the Nolan, the burden of whose thought is "let us be tolerant of antipa-

34. Ibid., pp. 145–46.

thies." Joyce illustrates the reconciliation (or "helixtrolysis") of antipathies (or the even more ambiguous and contradictory "amboadipates") by having Professor Jones suddenly reveal that he, like Wyndham Lewis, is a painter as well as a philosopher: "Every admirer has seen my goulache of Marge." Jones's portrait in gouache, *The Very Picture of a Needlesswoman,* is at the same time an abstract canvas and a portrait. Joyce here refers to a painting reproduced in *Blast,* no. 1, Lewis's *Portrait of an Englishwoman,* whose abstract arrangement of geometric forms in tilting cubist planes suggests a portrait only if one calls it, as Jones does, a portrait of "Rhomba, lady Trabezond." Like Lewis's portrait, Jones's is geometric, a triangle, which Ezra Pound called the "central life-form" of Lewis's Vorticist works.[35] In themselves Burrus and Caseous comprise an "isocelating biangle" which needs the subject of the portrait, the "Needlesswoman" Marge, to complete the triangular form and reconcile space and time. Thus the moral is the same as in the tale of the Mookse and the Gripes: Nuvoletta in the former and Marge in the latter are needed to fulfill the potentials of Burrus and Caseous or the Mookse and the Gripes.

The fable of Burrus and Caseous, however, shows that it is Lewis's artistic intolerance that spoils the possible reconciliation. When Burrus and Caseous ignore Marge because they are too busy arguing, she leaves them for another man. Jones-Lewis learns nothing by his creation of Marge's portrait and can only cry, "Alick and alack!" that Marge should be as receptive to Caseous as she is to Burrus. Joyce's temporal art of narrative uses one of Lewis's own spatial

35. Ezra Pound, *Gaudier-Brzeska: A Memoir* (New York: New Directions, 1970), p. 137. For a further explanation of this passage in *Finnegans Wake,* see my "Portrait of Lady Trabezond," *A Wake Newslitter* 13 (October 1976):98–99.

creations, the Vorticist portrait of a lady, to show Lewis, if he only had eyes to see, that Joyce alone is "tolerant of antipathies" and striving for an art that transcends space and time.

Although the principal attacks on Lewis as space man are found in these fables of the Ondt, Mookse, and Burrus, Joyce continued to return Lewis's fire in other sections of "Work in Progress" and the completed *Finnegans Wake.* When *The Enemy,* no. 3, equated Joyce's and Gertrude Stein's "polygluttonous" style, Joyce replied by playing on Stein's name (*stein,* stone) and describing an irate critic of HCE who "drunkishly pegged a few glatt stones, all of a size, by way of final mocks for his grapes" (p. 72). Lewis also used his own creative works to carry on the battle, as when a character in *The Childermass* says a man called Belcanto (Joyce) "becomes rather abusive sometimes when he discovers me talking about him—but as it's in his bellocanto cant it's as though you were being called *no gentleman* or *you're another* in singsong pedlar's french."[36]

Joyce also used the *Wake* to snipe at T. S. Eliot, editor of the "Craterium" (p. 150), and the "confusianist" Ezra Pound (p. 131). Professor Jones's pose of universal culture (one of his fables is in his own "easyfree translation" from the Javanese) is related by one critic to Ezra Pound's cross-cultural pretentions, and another notes how prophetic Joyce's description of the sounds of a radio, "sounds pound . . . electrically filtered," seems when one thinks of Pound's broadcasts on Italian radio during World War II.[37] This reference to Pound's political involvement suggests the basic conflict between Joyce and the Vortex. As Joyce wrote in 1928, "The more

---

36. Lewis, *Childermass,* p. 278.
37. David Hayman, "Pound at the Wake, or the Uses of a Contemporary," *James Joyce Quarterly* 2 (Spring 1964):209; Read, ed., *Pound/Joyce,* p. 264.

I hear of the political, philosophical, ethical zeal and labours of Pound's big brass band the more I wonder I was ever let into it 'with my magic flute'."[38] Pound's zeal was of course nothing to ridicule; nor were the philosophical and ethical passions of Wyndham Lewis and T. S. Eliot. Yet Joyce's misgivings were justified; a "brassy" quality certainly infected many of Lewis's and Pound's works. Although Joyce is often characterized as an apolitical writer, he had profound political intuitions that served him better than Pound's and Lewis's passionate convictions served them.[39] The developing political spirit of Pound, Eliot, and Lewis can be traced through their reactions to the development of Joyce's art. They had many reasons for objecting to Joyce's work in progress, including sheer bafflement, but the ground bass of their objections was political.

In the twenties, Pound's praise of *Ulysses* was unshadowed by any social or political misgivings. He saw the novel as a satire on the bourgeoisie, as an updated and even more

38. Joyce, *Letters,* vol. 1, p. 277.
39. Joyce is studied neither in John Harrison's five essays in *The Reactionaries* (New York: Schocken Books, 1967) nor in George Panichas's anthology of twenty-two essays, *The Politics of Twentieth-Century Novelists* (New York: Hawthorne Books, 1971). In Panichas's volume, various writers briefly praise Joyce as a man who "rose superior" to the "lure of politics" as well as deprecate him as a devotee of an "apolitical, myth-minded cult of art." Panichas implicitly reveals why no single essay on Joyce appears in his volume when he refers to Joyce's "aesthetic approach" and his "remoteness from the human spectacle." In his *Political Identities of Ezra Pound and T. S. Eliot* (Stanford: Stanford University Press, 1973), Richard Chace refers to Joyce's "apolitical stance." A well-known Joyce scholar, Philip F. Herring, examines this reputed "apolitical stance" in his essay "Joyce's Politics," in *New Light on Joyce from the Dublin Symposium,* ed. Fritz Senn (Bloomington: Indiana University Press, 1972), and comes to a judgment even harsher than Ezra Pound's of Joyce's lack of interest in social matters, which Herring says amounted to "an illness that prevented him from meeting other men as equals in an atmosphere of mutual trust [and] prevented him from seeing the world as anything more than grist for the mill of his art."

elaborate *Bouvard et Pécuchet*. Eliot also emphasized the social significance of *Ulysses* when he wrote that it was "the most important expression which the present age has found" and praised its "classical" (a word he used more flexibly than Lewis) attempt to give "a shape and a significance to the immense panorama of futility and anarchy which is contemporary history."[40] Like Ezra Pound, Eliot reads his own disgust with the modern world into Joyce's more tolerant world view. *Ulysses* contains decent people such as Martin Cunningham and Leopold Bloom himself as well as mean-spirited wastelanders such as Mr. Deasy and The Citizen. Pound in particular mistook Joyce's basically affirmative view of Leopold Bloom, the bourgeois Jew.

Lewis understood *Ulysses* better than Eliot or Pound did. He was the first critic to put the relative significance of Stephen and Bloom in perspective when he wrote that Bloom "wins the reader's sympathy every time he appears; and he never is confronted with the less and less satisfactory Dedalus (in the beau rôle) without the latter losing trick after trick to his disreputable rival."[41] (Even Lewis, however, fails to realize how carefully Joyce calculates this very effect.) Despite Lewis's appreciation of Bloom and his obsession with temporal art, his approach to *Ulysses* is as essentially social or political as Eliot's or Pound's. In a passage Pound thought memorable, Lewis wrote that *Ulysses* "is like a gigantic victorian quilt or antimacassar. Or it is the voluminous curtain that fell, belated (with the alarming momentum of a ton or two of personally organized rubbish), upon the victorian scene. So rich was its delivery, its pent-up outpour-

40. Eliot, "Ulysses, Order and Myth," in *Selected Prose of T. S. Eliot,* ed. Frank Kermode (New York: Harcourt Brace Jovanovich, 1975), pp. 175, 177.
41. Lewis, *Time and Western Man,* p. 117.

ing so vehement, that it will remain, eternally cathartic, a monument like a record diarrhoea."[42] One can scarcely tell from this passage that Lewis admired *Ulysses* as a satiric masterpiece. This admiration nevertheless shows through in the description of the work's "eternally cathartic" social satire. When Lewis could not find this social awareness in "Work in Progress"—an awareness he already thought weakened by *Ulysses'* nostalgia for the past—Lewis concluded that Joyce was "as bourgeois as a goldmedalled spaniel."[43]

Pound had also changed his mind about Joyce by the time he refused to publish a section of "Work in Progress" in *The Exile*. He was amused by early fragments of the *Wake*, and wrote in 1931 that "I thoroughly approve of Mr. Joyce making experiments." But as the experiments were prolonged, Pound complained that Joyce's work implied a "passive acceptance" of society's evils and that Joyce himself was a "small bourgeois, to the UTMOST."[44] Pound thought that Joyce, ironically like Pound's own Hugh Selwyn Mauberley, was "out of date," that "Joyce's mind has been deprived of Joyce's eyesight for too long . . . Joyce knows very little of life as it has been in the large since he finished *Ulysses*."[45] Pound had Lewis's criticism of *Ulysses* in mind when he wrote to Lewis about possible contributors to a new journal, ". . . no need of *transition* crap or Jheezus in progress. I am about thru with that diarrhoea of consciousness."[46]

Eliot too became disenchanted with Joyce because of *Finnegans Wake*, although he loyally saw to it that Faber

42. Ibid., p. 109.
43. Lewis, *Childermass*, p. 176.
44. Read, ed., *Pound/Joyce*, pp. 239, 251, 268.
45. Ibid., p. 256.
46. Ibid., p. 257.

published what he called a "monstrous masterpiece."[47] He thought that Joyce had retreated from the social world into an egocentric world of his own consciousness and compared the blind poet John Milton to the nearly blind Joyce. Like Pound, Eliot suggests that Joyce's weak sight has conditioned his art, for it "shows a turning from the visible world to draw rather on the resources of phantasmagoria." Eliot compares Milton and Joyce in the very terms Lewis favored: "What I find in *Work in Progress* is an auditory imagination abnormally sharpened at the expense of the visual." With a tactless play on words, Eliot concludes that Joyce's work could lead literature into a "blind alley."[48]

Lewis obviously disapproved of *Finnegans Wake* for reasons that were complicated by his rivalry with Joyce, which the poets Eliot and Pound felt less sharply, though they knew that *The Waste Land* and *The Cantos* existed in the shadow of *Ulysses*. Yet his basic objection is no different from Pound's. This objection is expressed in *The Childermass* when a character named Master Joys is asked to justify himself as a writer. Lewis imagines the following reply: "As for that cross-word polyglottony in the which I indulges misself for recreation bighorror, why bighorror isn't it aysy the aysiest way right out of what you might call the postoddydeucian dam dirty cul of a sack into which shure and bighorrer I've bin and gone and thropped misself."[49] Lewis's parody implies that Joyce refuses to fight (Pound's "passive acceptance") the "cul of a sack" that is modern culture, and so is in effect saying "ay" (taking the "aysiest way") to its disintegration. As a result, Joyce's work is mere "recreation"

47. Eliot, "The Frontiers of Criticism," in *On Poetry and Poets* (New York: Farrar, Straus & Giroux, 1961), p. 120.
48. Eliot, "Milton, I," in *Selected Prose,* pp. 262–63.
49. Lewis, *Childermass,* p. 175.

and not the criticism of culture that great art should be and that *Ulysses* was. Master Joys's claim that he writes for "recreation" is also an allusion to Joyce's connection with *transition* and to the reply to Lewis's *Enemy* attacks that its editors made in 1927:

> If we have a warm feeling for both [the Surrealists] and the Communists it is because the movements which they represent are aimed at the destruction of a thoroughly rotten structure. . . . Contemporary society seems to us to be in an abysmally dark state and we are entertained intellectually, if not physically, with the idea of its destruction. . . . Our interests are confined to literature and life. . . . It is our purpose purely and simply to amuse ourselves.[50]

In Lewis's eyes, *transition*'s pose of detached amusement masks the same kind of social nihilism that he discovers in Joyce's work.

The Vortex's criticism of Joyce is distorted by numerous ironic overtones. Ezra Pound, for example, wrote in 1914 that Joyce's "most engaging merit" was that "he carefully avoids telling you a lot you don't want to know. . . . He does not believe 'life' would be all right if we stopped vivisection or if we instituted a new sort of 'economics.'"[51] Such praise now sounds strange from the author of the repetitive economic episodes ("sounds pound") of *The Cantos*. One is similarly surprised when the creator of the "Sweeney" poems writes of the creator of Leopold Bloom and the many politically exploited members of Dublin's lower middle class that Joyce "did not compose a novel through direct interest in, and sympathy with, other human beings, but by enlarging his own consciousness so as to include them." The weakness

50. Jolas, Paul, and Sage, "First Aid to the Enemy," p. 21.
51. Pound, *Literary Essays,* p. 400.

of this judgment is especially obvious when Eliot goes on to say, making in 1943 the mistake that Lewis avoided in 1927, that Joyce introduced "himself" into *Ulysses* as Stephen Dedalus and his "opposite" as Leopold Bloom.[52] The prototype for these ironies is Lewis's attack on Joyce for creating a "time-book" when Lewis himself could not "beat time."

Yet even if the Vortex did mistake Joyce's aims and sympathies, their case against Joyce's political passivity still stands. To defend Joyce successfully against their charges one needs a standard by which the social awareness of all four writers can be measured. The difficulty is to find a standard common not only to Joyce and the Vortex but also to Eliot the Anglo-Catholic, Pound the monetary reformer and supporter of Italian Fascism, and Lewis, by turns the Fascist sympathizer, internationalist, and socialist.

The work of Julien Benda may provide such a standard. Pound's and Lewis's admiration for the French political thinker at least gives a useful context for judging their political involvement. In 1927 Benda published *La Trahison des clercs,* which Lewis called a "modern classic." Benda's *clercs,* who set the intellectual and ethical standards of cultural life, are of two 'types. The first type, such as Leonardo da Vinci or René Descartes, disdains politics altogether; the second, such as Erasmus or Chateaubriand, involves himself with politics but with "a generalizing of feeling, a disdain for immediate results."[53] The "treasonous" intellectuals, such as Charles Maurras, Rudyard Kipling, and Gabriele d'Annunzio in modern times, are those whose

52. Eliot, "The Approach to James Joyce," *Listener* 30 (October 14, 1943):447.
53. Julien Benda, *The Great Betrayal* [La Trahison des clercs], trans. Richard Aldington (London: George Routledge, 1928), p. 32.

passionate espousal of causes destroys the traditional objectivity of the *clerc*. Instead of judging political events by ideal standards, these intellectuals allow politics to dictate their standards. Benda honors the detachment of such a *clerc* as da Vinci and defends him against the false intellectual whose "literature is filled with his contempt for the man who shuts himself up with art or science and takes no interest in the passions of the State. He is violently on the side of Michaelangelo crying shame upon Leonardo da Vinci for his indifference to the misfortunes of Florence, and against the master of the Last Supper when he replied that indeed the study of beauty occupied his whole heart."[54]

As one of Benda's critics observes, the irony of Benda's position is that he is no detached intellectual himself "but an eager and redoubtable polemicist, exactly like some of the '*clercs*' he attacked so sharply for their betrayal."[55] Benda's use of the emotive word "treason" is itself an indication of his self-contradictory passion. Yet this contradiction does not invalidate his position or lessen his influence.

As Geoffrey Wagner has shown, Lewis conceived of himself as a *clerc* in Benda's sense of the term. Wagner notes that Lewis's claims of detachment and objectivity stretch from the 1915 *Blast,* in which he calls himself "an IMPARTIAL MAN in times of war," to his stand as an "independent observer" in 1926, to his claim in 1931 that he thinks "nonpolitically in everything, in complete detachment," and then to his later avowals that he is "alone among writers today in advocating no partisanship in the political field" (1934) and that "politically I stand nowhere" (1950).[56] Lewis of course

54. Ibid., pp. 32–33.
55. Robert J. Niess, *Julien Benda* (Ann Arbor: University of Michigan Press, 1956), p. 174.
56. Quoted in Wagner, *Wyndham Lewis,* pp. 18–19.

protests too much; like Benda, he was really passionately involved in political issues. Although he did not, like Pound, use his creative works to propagandize his social beliefs, he was, as T. S. Eliot called him, a "dispossessed artist." Like Eliot, he felt that he had to attack the forces corrupting his culture if it were to become capable of understanding and supporting true art. This effort deflected his creative energies, as he himself constantly complained, into criticism. He wrote with haste and ill temper, as if politics and society were really unworthy of his attention. Lewis, Pound, and Eliot inherited the belief of the 1890s that art justified society and not the other way around. But they also inherited the politically engaged tradition of writers from Dickens to Coleridge. The result was what Richard Chace calls "an awkward emergence from the Symbolist quarantine."[57]

Not only did politics sap Lewis's energies and damage his reputation; it eventually set the terms for his creative works. Even in *The Revenge for Love* (1937), which most of his critics consider his greatest novel, Lewis's disgust with foreign involvement in pre–Civil War Spain reduces most of his characters to mere villainous manipulators or pitiable victims. The novel that I consider Lewis's greatest examines the dangers of political involvement. *Self Condemned* (1954) tells of René Harding (whose first name is an allusion to René Descartes), who resigns his chair of history on the eve of World War II and lives out the war in Canadian exile. His isolated and heroic attempt to understand the reality of historic events so embitters him that he loses his intellectual integrity. After years of poverty, he begins writing on political affairs for the press, delivers a popular lecture series at a provincial university, and reenters the academic world— having compromised his principles—a "glacial shell of a

57. Chace, *Political Identities,* p. xviii.

man." His tragedy is summed up in the words Lewis uses to describe Shakespeare's protagonists, whose "tragedy is that they are involved in a *real* action: whereas they come from, and naturally inhabit, an ideal world."[58] The "ideal world" for René is the world of the *clerc,* from which he is driven by the ungovernable passions of a world at war.

This theme of the *clerc*'s destruction continues in Lewis's characterization of James Pullman in *The Human Age.* Pullman slowly becomes involved in a literally diabolic political movement because only this movement will support him as a writer. (Lewis is thinking of Joyce's involvement with the *transition* nihilists.) This theme also dominates Lewis's final novel, *The Red Priest* (1956). His main character is again a false *clerc*—indeed, a cleric, Father Augustine Card. Father Card shocks his fashionable High Church congregation by calling for direct political action and by embracing communism. The suppressed violence of his nature finally destroys him after he accidentally kills a fellow priest in a scuffle. His own death as a missionary, which he becomes in expiation for his part in the accident, is also violent and again the result of leaving the world of thought for that of action. Lewis's own bitter reflections on the meaning of his embattled career emerge from the strange final sentences of *The Red Priest.* Father Card's widow gives the son who is born after his father's death "the fearful name of Zero. She could see that he would look like his terrible father; that he was fated to blast his way across space and time."[59] From *Self Condemned* to the last words of his final novel, Lewis's fiction laments the career of a "dispossessed artist."

When Pound moved from London to Paris in 1920, Julien

58. Lewis, *The Lion and the Fox: The Rôle of the Hero in the Plays of Shakespeare* (1927; reprinted London: Methuen, 1951), p. 187.
59. Lewis, *The Red Priest* (London: Methuen, 1956), p. 298.

Benda was the one writer who convinced him of Paris's superior "mental life." Pound recommended Benda to Eliot and praised him for his "hardness" and his "patience of analysis for which I can cite no contemporary parallel north of the Channel."[60] Later in his career, Pound refers to Benda in Canto 91, which begins with the magnificent invocation to Pound's historical muse,

> that the body of light come forth
> from the body of fire . . .

Pages of great lyric poetry follow until, with one of the startling juxtapositions that is the delight and sometimes the despair of Pound's readers, a strident, italicized passage intervenes:

> *Democracies electing their sewage*
> *till there is no clear thought about holiness*
> *a dung flow from 1913*
> *and, in this, their kikery functioned, Marx, Freud,*
> *and the american beaneries*
> *Filth under filth,*
> > *Maritain, Hutchins,*
> *or as Benda remarked: "La trahison" . . .*

Pound seems to remember only Benda's title, for this passage virtually rejects the thesis of *La Trahison*. Pound attacks Freud and Jacques Maritain because they are *clercs* who are leading people into what he considers psychological and philosophical byways that are unrelated to the new direction Pound wants society to take. Pound misuses Benda in the

60. In a letter of July 3, 1920, Eliot tells Pound that he is not sure who Benda is but that he intends to read him (Beinecke Library, Yale University); Pound (signed: "B.L."), "Julien Benda," *Athenaeum* 95 (July 9, 1920):62.

same way in a letter he wrote to Lewis in 1936 to urge "the Vort" to "direct action": "time for concerted action IS. Manifesto against TREASON of the CLERKS."[61]

The passage from Canto 91, with its slur about the "kikery" of Marx and Freud, shows the consequences of passionate involvement in political issues for Pound. This passage and many as bad throughout *The Cantos* cannot cancel out its great poetry, but the passion that produced it does destroy the insight into history that Pound had early in his career. In *A Draft of XXX Cantos* (1930), Pound's analysis of the forces that corrupted Renaissance art and society gives his work greater epic reach than it was ever to attain again. In the section that followed *XXX Cantos, Eleven New Cantos* (1937), Mussolini appears as a fiscal liberator and Pound's credit as a poet who can illuminate the fate of a culture is bankrupt. The closer he comes to the contemporary world, in which he is breathlessly pursuing a political and economic program, the more naive and irrelevant his epic themes become and the less able he is to see the universal patterns of growth and decay he revealed in the Renaissance. As Eliot observes, "When he deals with antiquities, he extracts the essentially living; when he deals with contemporaries, he sometimes notes only the accidental."[62] Nothing can destroy Pound's lyric gift or diminish the courage that made him take great risks for his art. But there is no denying the sad irony that he betrays the mission of the *clerc* in the very act of denouncing *la trahison*.

T. S. Eliot's view of the relationship of the artist to the events of the day is more complex, or at least more compli-

---

61. Pound to Lewis, October 29, 1936 ("Anno XIV"), Olin Library, Cornell University.

62. Eliot, "Introduction," in *Ezra Pound: Selected Poems,* ed. T. S. Eliot (London: Faber & Faber, 1928), p. xiii.

cated, than Pound's or Lewis's. In his review of Benda's *Trahison,* Eliot contrasts Benda's ideal of the *clerc* to Wyndham Lewis's practice as an artist and social critic and praises Lewis's relative involvement with social issues. Eliot dislikes Benda's "romantic view of critical detachment" because he thinks that it makes the artist socially irrelevant: "Where there is no vital connection [with society], the man may be a brilliant virtuoso, but is probably nothing more."[63] Eliot's disapproval of Joyce's *Wake,* of which "large stretches . . . are, without elaborate explanation, merely beautiful nonsense," is based on this distrust of the mere "virtuoso."[64]

Unlike Lewis and Pound, Eliot did not allow his involvement in social issues to sap or divert his creativity, although his editing of *The Criterion* did burden him during his most creative period. Eliot's criticism, on the other hand, suffers at times from his attempting a "vital connection" with society, as in the well-known excesses of *After Strange Gods* (1934), in which Gerard Manley Hopkins is criticized for not furthering the struggle against liberalism, in which D. H. Lawrence is described as a "very sick man indeed," and in which Eliot says that in a traditional society "reasons of race and religion combine to make any large number of free-thinking Jews undesirable."[65] Of course, Eliot later regretted such remarks and refused to let *After Strange Gods* be reprinted. It is nevertheless significant that in a work in which he specifically adopts the socially conscious "role of a moralist,"[66] he writes some of his most irresponsible criticism. Eliot noted that Benda did not practice the objectivity

63. Eliot, "The Idealism of Julien Benda," *New Republic* 62 (December 12, 1928):107.
64. Eliot, "Frontiers of Criticism," p. 120.
65. Eliot, *After Strange Gods: A Primer of Modern Heresy* (New York: Harcourt, Brace, 1934), p. 20.
66. Ibid., p. 10.

he preached and that "he fell into treason while accusing others."[67] There is a similar irony in the moralism of *After Strange Gods,* which is in a sense Eliot's own *Trahison des clercs.*

One cannot say that every artist should follow Benda's principles if he wishes to protect his art from corrupting influences. Benda's *clerc* should neither be revered as an ideal nor summarily dismissed as being, as Jean-Paul Sartre claims he is, "always on the side of the oppressors."[68] One can say, however, that the closer Pound, Eliot, and Lewis came to Benda's principles, the better critics they became. Eliot made great contributions to his culture when he implicitly followed Benda's ideal as editor of *The Criterion,* which was a more positive achievement than Lewis's *Enemy* or Pound's *Exile* because it avoided the one-man rigor of those journals. In 1936 Eliot expressed the Benda-like principle that guided his editorship when he commented on a series of French manifestos against Italy's invasion of Abyssinia:

> If—what is often doubted—there remains any place for quarterly reviews in the modern world, their task is surely to concern themselves with political philosophy, rather than with politics, and with the examination of the fundamental ideas of philosophies rather than with the problems of application. But whenever any collection of individuals, of *clercs,* takes upon itself to issue a manifesto at some moment of crisis, then I think that it is within our province to discuss, not so much the crisis itself, as the opinions of the intellectuals about it.[69]

The idea of the *clerc* became increasingly important to Eliot in such works as *The Idea of a Christian Society* (1940) and

67. Eliot, "Idealism of Julien Benda," p. 107.
68. Jean-Paul Sartre, *Literature and Existentialism,* trans. Bernard Frechtman (New York: Citadel Press, 1964), p. 157.
69. Eliot, "A Commentary," *Criterion* 15 (January 1936):265–69.

his play *The Confidential Clerk* (1954). He defines the *clerc* in the play when Lady Elizabeth tells Colby, the confidential clerk of the title, that he should associate with "intellectual, well-bred people / of spirituality."[70] Despite his increasing conformance with Benda's principles, Eliot forgot Benda's distinction between the two kinds of true *clerc*. In a talk he gave in 1944, Eliot confessed that he could not find his copy of *La Trahison* and said that Benda, "as I remember, seemed to expect everybody to be a sort of Spinoza."[71] Spinoza is indeed a *clerc* of Benda's first type, such as da Vinci, who disdains politics altogether; but there is also the second type, such as Erasmus or Zola, who treats political events with a "generalizing of feeling, a disdain for immediate results," as Eliot and even Lewis could treat them when at their best. Eliot followed Benda better than he knew in his later career, just as Lewis and Pound followed Benda less wisely than they knew.

James Joyce expressed no opinion of his French contemporary Julien Benda—not even, so far as anyone can tell, in *Finnegans Wake*. But Richard Ellmann has recorded that Joyce attended a party where "most of the company gathered around another guest, Julien Benda, who was denouncing to Adrienne Monnier her friends Valéry, Claudel, and Gide, while she defended them with equal vigor."[72] Joyce left the debate and went off to another room to look at a book. He had the temperament of the true *clerc* and had the right to

70. Eliot, *The Confidential Clerk* (New York: Harcourt, Brace, 1954), p. 82.
71. Eliot, "On the Place and Function of the Clerisy: A Paper Written by T. S. Eliot for Discussion at the Moot Meeting of December 1944," in Roger Kojecky, *T. S. Eliot's Social Criticism* (New York: Farrar, Straus & Giroux, 1971), p. 246.
72. Ellmann, *James Joyce*, p. 503.

laugh at Pound and Lewis when he wrote to Harriet Weaver, "I am afraid poor Mr. Hitler-Missler will soon have few admirers in Europe apart from your nieces and my nephews, Masters W. Lewis and E. Pound."[73] When Mussolini invaded Abyssinia, Joyce wrote to his daughter-in-law about Pound's politics: "May the 17 devils take Muscoloni and the Alibiscindians! Why don't they make Pound commander-in-chief for Bagonghi and elect me Negus of Amblyopia?"[74]

As these quotations suggest, Joyce avoided the political excesses of Eliot, Pound, and Lewis. Yet this fact does not fully answer the Vortex's criticism of his disengagement. Perhaps Joyce avoided their mistakes only because he was unconcerned about the great problems of his age. One might even be offended by his insouciant reference to the invasion of Abyssinia. Eliot wrote that there is "a kind of scepticism which is caused merely by the refusal to think things out,"[75] and one could argue that Joyce's remarks on Hitler and Mussolini betray such easy skepticism.

A skeptic Joyce surely was, but I do not believe this quality was merely negative; it allowed him to view the passions of his age critically. This account of the Vortex's political involvement necessarily refers to the widespread anti-Semitism in modern literary culture. Pound was obviously guilty of this cruelly dangerous passion, and to Eliot's remark about "free-thinking Jews" one can add the unpleasant Jewish characters, such as Julius Ratner, in Lewis's fiction. It was Joyce who sensed the dangerous potential of anti-Semitism when he caricatured the anti-Semite Mr. Deasy in *Ulysses* and created the Jew Leopold Bloom, the Dublin scapegoat. Here one can say of Joyce, as

73. Joyce, *Letters,* 3:311.
74. Ibid., 1:381.
75. Quoted in Kojecky, *T. S. Eliot's Social Criticism,* p. 90.

is said of the finder of ALP's "mamafesta," that his "socio-scientific sense is sound as a bell, sir."[76] Somehow Joyce saw the universal patterns of oppression emerging long before his contemporaries, and nowhere are such patterns better charted than in *Finnegans Wake.*

A look at the opening pages of the *Wake* reveals the "vital connection" that Joyce forged with the world by treating historical events with Benda's "generalizing of feeling." The *Wake*'s reader is, within a few pages of the opening, guided into the "Willingdone Museyroom" of military history (from which one exits feet first) to learn of the battles of Clontarf and Waterloo. Throughout the work these battles stand for the destructive recurrence of conflicts in what Stephen Dedalus calls the "nightmare of history." The results of the nightmare are the human debris of battle: "spattees and flasks of all nations, clavicures and scampulars . . . foder allmicheal and a lugly parson of cates and howitzer muchears and midgers and maggets."[77] As in the Shem/Shaun pattern, the conflicts are irreconcilable. The battle Joyce describes between Willingdone and Lipoleum issues only in slaughter, just as the conflict of the Danes and the Irish at Clontarf result in a "dungtarf" of bodies. The invading Danes (the Shaun figure Jute) will not heed the native Irish (the Shem figure Mutt) any more than the Ondt will listen to the Gracehoper's song, even when Mutt shows the invader the recurring futility of war through a metaphor borrowed from Book 12 of the *Iliad*: "Countlessness of livestories have netherfallen by this plage, flick as flowflakes, litters from aloft, like a waast wizzard all of whirlworlds. Now are all tombed to the mound, isges to isges, erde from erde. Pride,

76. *Finnegans Wake*, p. 112.
77. Ibid., p. 11.

O pride, thy prize!"[78] Joyce's understanding of the tragic recurrence of violence in the vortical "whirlworlds" of human experience underlies the gaiety of the language. In *Finnegans Wake,* Joyce records his effort to awake from what Stephen Dedalus called the "nightmare of history."

To counter Pound's and Lewis's claims that Joyce was unaware of contemporary events, one could cite the many references to them that Bernard Benstock assembles in *Joyce-again's Wake,* or Richard Ellmann's demonstration that the space/time dichotomy underlies Joyce's attack on the state's dominance of space and the church's attempt to rule over time and eternity.[79] Nor is the reputed inaccessibility of Joyce's work at issue, or at any rate it should not be where the authors of such formidable works as *The Cantos, Ash Wednesday,* and *The Childermass* are concerned. As Joyce writes after the Mutt and Jute episode, "If you are abcedminded . . . what curios of signs" a reader can find "in this alaphbed! Can you rede . . . its world? It is the same told of all."[80] This tale "told of all," a history of mankind, is in fact the same "tale of the tribe" that Pound attempts to narrate in *The Cantos.*

One merely needed some patience and objectivity to see what Joyce was doing, as he himself told his puzzled readers. When Shem defends ALP's "mamafesta," and by implication the *Wake,* he observes that "patience is the great thing"; and

78. Ibid., p. 17.
79. Bernard Benstock, *Joyce-again's Wake* (Seattle: University of Washington Press, 1965), pt. 1, chap. 2; Richard Ellmann, *The Consciousness of James Joyce* (New York: Oxford University Press, 1977), p. 80. I am grateful to John Shoptaw of the University of Missouri–Columbia for discussing this issue with me and for pointing out relevant passages in *Finnegans Wake.*
80. *Finnegans Wake,* p. 18.

with Pound's irritable insistence on Confucian calm and practicality in mind, he warns that patience is especially useful for "worried business folk who may not have had many momentums to master Kung's doctrine of the meang." Joyce is also answering Pound's criticisms when Shem says of the "mamafesta": "To conclude purely negatively from the positive absence of political odia and monetary requests that its page cannot ever have been a penproduct of a man or woman of that period or those parts is only one more unlookedfor conclusion leaped at."[81]

Joyce apparently received, as Lewis often did, one of Pound's many letters urging his friends to "direct action." Near the climax of one of Shaun's denunciations of Shem, Shaun-Pound says, "Why not take direct action," and claims that "the word is my Wife, to exponse and expound."[82] Joyce's reply to such an arrogant request, through the voice of the father figure HCE, sums up his general reply to the Vortex: "—I mean to sit here on this altknoll where you are now, Surly guy, replete in myself, as long as I live, in my homespins, like a sleepingtop, with all that's buried ofsins insince insensed insidesofme. If I can't upset this pound of pressed ollaves I can sit up zounds of sounds upon him."[83] Although Joyce may not appear to move from his own provincial home ground, he is in fact on the "altknoll" of universal history, "replete" in a wisdom that extends beyond contemporary events. Although his mental activity may seem like passivity, his consciousness of his buried wisdom is intense as he lives in his "homespins, like a sleepingtop." With this perhaps unconscious reference to a Vortex image, Joyce delivers his ultimate defense of his world view. He was

81. Ibid., p. 108.
82. Ibid., p. 167.
83. Ibid., p. 499.

not trapped by the polarities of the historical situation any more than Henri Gaudier was by those of the Vorticist art world. Joyce followed his own advice to Lewis, which he expressed in one of the *Wake*'s infrequent passages of plain English: "Let us be tolerant of antipathies." It was Joyce rather than Pound, Eliot, or Lewis who was at the still center of the vortex of history.

7

The Point of the Vortex

there is our norm of spirit

our　中　chung

—Ezra Pound, Canto 84

The Vorticist is at his maximum point of energy when stillest.
　　　　　　　　　　　　　—Wyndham Lewis in *Blast*

Ezra Pound and Wyndham Lewis never ceased lamenting
the hopes blasted in 1914. Their expectation of a modern
renaissance was not unique to the Vortex, but their disappointment in not achieving it was unusually intense. Such
writers as John Galsworthy, Sir Edward Marsh, and Laurence Binyon hoped in 1910 for a glorious new Georgian age
in literature to coincide with the death of Edward VII, the
last clearly visible link to the Victorian age. Moved by a
"sense of things coming out right," Clive Bell began to write
a book on the arts called *The New Renaissance* in 1910.[1] If
these writers were as cruelly disappointed by World War I as
Pound, Eliot, and Lewis, they were less directly affected by
it. The Vortex was of the generation that fought and died in
the war, a circumstance that intensified their reaction to it
even when, as with Pound and Eliot, they did not themselves
go to war. Moreover, Pound, Eliot, and Lewis were not so
naive about the nature of the conflict as were still younger

1. K. K. Ruthven, *A Guide to Ezra Pound's Personae* (Berkeley and
Los Angeles: University of California Press, 1969), pp. 16–17; Clive Bell,
Old Friends (New York: Harcourt, Brace, 1956), p. 80.

members of the war generation, such as Henri Gaudier (in 1914, Lewis was thirty-two and Gaudier twenty-three years old). The divergent attitudes toward war are clear from Gaudier's belief that the war was a "great remedy" and Lewis's that "'this "great war" is the beginning of a period, far from it being a war-that-will-end-war.'"[2]

Lewis believed that the war crushed all "surplus vigor" as well as the "will to play" from modern civilization, and Pound believed that "the minute the war was OVER England sank into black mud."[3] Gaudier's death was the tragic sign of this descent into mud and blackness. Charles Olson thought that "it is as though Pound has never got over it, that Gaudier's death is the source of his hate for Contemporary England and America, that then, in 1915, his attack on democracy got mixed up with Gaudier's death."[4] Olson's impression is verified in a letter of 1949 in which Pound told Lewis that he got over his "Walter Scott" romantic phase and developed "serious curiosity startin @ death of Gaudier."[5] Lewis's rage at Gaudier's death was still burning in 1937, when he wrote in his novel *The Revenge for Love* of the artist Victor Stamp, who dies uselessly for a political cause he does not understand.

Olson thought that Pound "only experienced war and politics once: in England, World War I."[6] This insight

2. Henri Gaudier, "Vortex Gaudier-Brzeska," *Blast,* no. 2, in Ezra Pound, *Gaudier-Brzeska: A Memoir* (New York: New Directions, 1970), p. 27. Lewis's sentiments are spoken by his character Rob Cairn in "The French Poodle," in *Unlucky for Pringle: Unpublished and Other Stories,* ed. C. J. Fox and Robert T. Chapman (London: Vision Press, 1973), p. 56. This story was first published in 1916.
3. Pound to Lewis, n.d. (1950s), Olin Library, Cornell University.
4. *Charles Olson and Ezra Pound: An Encounter at St. Elizabeths,* ed. Catherine Seelye (New York: Viking Press, 1975), p. 45.
5. Pound to Lewis, January 25, 1949, Olin Library, Cornell University.
6. *Charles Olson and Ezra Pound,* p. 44.

applies to Lewis as well and helps to account for his willingness to tolerate Hitler's rise until the late 1930s. Lewis himself has admitted that he indulged "in efforts at 'appeasement' beside which those of Mr. Chamberlain pale in comparison."[7] As for Eliot's reaction to the war, Lewis memorably describes at least one motive for Eliot's wasteland distress: "He was an American who was in flight from the same thing that kept Pound over here, and with what had he been delected, as soon as he had firmly settled himself on this side of the water? The spectacle of Europe committing suicide—just that."[8] Lewis wrote in 1934 that the true artist must be "penetrated by a sense of the great discontinuity of our destiny."[9] The theme of discontinuity goes back to T. E. Hulme's prewar theory that contemporary man was living through "the breaking up of an era." Hulme was optimistic about the new, postrenaissance period that he believed was forming and could not know that the breaking-up process would end his life in a gun pit in France. Pound thought that Vorticism's strength was that it registered the breakup: "While all other periodicals were whispering PEACE in one tone or another . . . BLAST alone dared to present the actual discords of modern civilization, DISCORDS now only too apparent in the open conflict between teutonic atavism and unsatisfactory Democracy."[10] Pound himself proclaimed the discontinuity of the era when he placed his "END OF CHRISTIAN ERA" banner in the Rebel Art Centre.

7. Wyndham Lewis, *The Hitler Cult* (1939; reprinted New York: Gordon Press, 1972), p. viii.

8. Lewis, "Early London Environment," in *T. S. Eliot: A Collection of Critical Essays,* ed. Hugh Kenner (Englewood Cliffs, N.J.: Prentice-Hall, 1962), p. 33.

9. Wyndham Lewis, *Men without Art* (London: Cassell, 1934), p. 126.

10. Ezra Pound, *Pavannes and Divagations* (New York: New Directions, 1958), p. 147.

Eliot defined this discord or discontinuity in his deceptively quiet observation that in the seventeenth century, following a civil war that drastically altered religious conditions, "a dissociation of sensibility set in, from which we have never recovered." Although a symptom of this "dissociation" is that the "ordinary man's experience is chaotic, irregular, fragmentary," the poet can still experience and express a "direct sensuous apprehension of thought."[11] Eliot's discussion of "dissociation" in 1921 uses the same general terms he used in his description of Wyndham Lewis in 1918 as an artist who unites intelligence with a "physical organism which interests itself directly in sensation for its own sake." Remarkably, Eliot praises Lewis's "perception of the world of immediate experience," a power that one knows from Eliot's dissertation on F. H. Bradley no mere mortal can possess. In this review of Lewis's first novel, *Tarr,* Eliot concludes that the artist is "more *primitive,* as well as more civilized than his contemporaries": "Primitive instincts and the acquired habits of ages are confounded in the ordinary man. In the work of Mr. Lewis we recognize the thought of the modern and the energy of the cave-man."[12] This conception of the artist as a primitive was dear to all of the original Vorticists and particularly to Gaudier, the "Savage Messiah." Lewis wrote in *Blast* that "the artist of the modern movement is a savage. . . . This enormous, jangling, journalistic, fairy desert of modern life serves him as Nature did more technically primitive man."[13]

T. E. Hulme recognized this link between primitivism and modernism when he defended Jacob Epstein's yoking of

11. T. S. Eliot, "The Metaphysical Poets," in *Selected Essays* (New York: Harcourt Brace Jovanovich, 1964), pp. 247–48.
12. T. S. Eliot, "Tarr," *Egoist* 5 (September 1918):105–6.
13. Lewis, *Wyndham Lewis on Art,* ed. Walter Michel and C. J. Fox (New York: Funk & Wagnalls, 1969), p. 28.

primitive motifs with semiabstract forms. In response to the charge that the sculptor's techniques were affectations, Hulme said that "in the peculiar conditions in which we find ourselves, which are really the breaking up of an era, it has again become quite possible for people here and there to have the attitude expressed by these formulae."[14] The artist of Hulme's new postrenaissance age was to have the unified sensibility that Eliot, though presumably not Hulme himself, detected in the era before the English Civil War. Pound found this sensibility in thirteenth-century Italy and said that he interested Hulme in his discovery that "Guido [Calvancanti] thought in accurate terms; that the phrases correspond to definite sensations undergone."[15] Pound also thought that this sensitivity to physical sensation was characteristic of primitive man. The connection between this primitivism and Imagist, or rather Vorticist, technique is neatly stated in Pound's essay on Vorticism: "An *image,* in our sense, is real because we know it directly."[16] We know it, that is, with a "subtle and instantaneous perception . . . such as savages and wild animals have of the necessities and dangers of the forest."[17]

At times Pound, Eliot, and Lewis wrote as if the dissociation of the modern age made art impossible; and at other times as if the artist, as opposed to the ordinary man, were still able to experience the world with a unified sensibility and so create art. When in a more positive mood, they

14. T. E. Hulme, "Mr. Epstein and the Critics," in *Further Speculations by T. E. Hulme,* ed. Sam Hynes (Minneapolis: University of Minnesota Press, 1955), p. 106.

15. Pound, *Literary Essays of Ezra Pound* (New York: New Directions, 1968), p. 162.

16. Pound, *Gaudier-Brzeska,* p. 86.

17. Pound, "Affirmations II. Vorticism," *New Age* 16 (January 14, 1915):278.

believed that the means of healing the breach lay in absorbing the Western tradition, unifying it within their own sensibilities, and becoming its spokesmen.

Not even the 1914 Vorticist wanted to jetison traditional art; the Vorticist painters merely wanted to junk the false tradition represented by portraits of fine ladies and race horses. The *Blast* manifesto concludes: "The nearest thing in England to a great traditional French artist, is a great revolutionary English one."[18] A respect for tradition was implicit in Pound's use of the term *Vorticism*. In 1912 he wrote that words were "great hollow cones of steel" charged with "the power of tradition, of centuries of race consciousness."[19] Speaking for the Vorticists, Pound explained, "We do not desire to evade comparison with the past. We prefer that the comparison be made by some intelligent person whose idea of 'the tradition' is not limited by the conventional taste of four or five centuries and one continent."[20] Pound, Eliot, and Lewis defended the Western tradition with their literary and social criticism—the most ambitious defense being Lewis's in *Time and Western Man.* In literary criticism, Pound noted, "Mr. Eliot and I are in complete agreement, or 'belong to the same school of critics', in so far as we both believe that the existing works form a complete order which is changed by the introduction of the 'really new' work."[21] With a heavy weight of allusions, the poetry of Eliot and Pound showed that they wrote "with a feeling that the whole of the literature of Europe . . . composes a simultaneous order." Thus behind Lewis's prose Eliot felt the "whole weight of the

18. *Wyndham Lewis on Art,* p. 31.
19. Pound, *Selected Prose, 1909–1965,* ed. William Cookson (New York: New Directions, 1973), p. 34.
20. Pound, *Gaudier-Brzeska,* p. 90.
21. Pound, "Praefatio," in *Active Anthology* (London: Faber & Faber, 1973), p. 9.

history of the language," particularly the prose of the Elizabethans.[22]

Within this general agreement on the living power of tradition there was room for much disagreement. For example, Lewis thought more highly of the age of William Hogarth and Thomas Rowlandson than did Pound or Eliot. Pound's spelling of the word *culture* as "kulchur," as if to disinfect it of associations with upper-class patrons of opening nights, indicates the chief disagreement between Pound and Eliot. When the Faber publishing firm was engaged in the trying task of editing Pound's *Guide to Kulchur,* Pound taunted one of the editors about the way "Possum" Eliot might react to his cross-cultural approach: "An how you gwine ter keep deh Possum in his feedbox when I brings in deh Chinas and blackmen??"[23] Pound also considered Lewis too emotionally involved in the dying Western tradition. Yet neither Eliot nor Lewis felt—any more than Pound did—that a defense of the Western tradition implied a neglect of foreign cultural traditions. Throughout his career, Lewis consistently praised Chinese and primitive art as superior to the naturalistic art of the West.

Lewis's criticism of Eliot and Pound's conception of culture was that it was too self-consciously the result of "the habits of the American university, spellbound by 'culture'."[24] Lewis himself wrote in a tradition that stems from Thomas Nash through Tobias Smollett and Charles Dickens, and this tradition remains deep in the texture and tone of his prose.

22. Eliot, "Tradition and the Individual Talent," in *Selected Essays,* p. 4; "The Three Provincialities," *Tyro,* no. 2 (1922), p. 13.

23. Quoted in Noel Stock, *The Life of Ezra Pound* (New York: Random House, 1970), p. 342.

24. Lewis, *The Letters of Wyndham Lewis,* ed. W. K. Rose (Norfolk, Conn.: New Directions, 1963), p. 224.

He objected to what he considered the display of scholarship in Eliot's and Pound's poetry and thought that Pound should have put down roots into his native culture. He wrote to Pound in 1946, "What a pity it is that the lure of history kept you locked up in the dusty old Mediterranean. The Hudson River Valley would have been a better place."[25]

This emphasis on tradition implies a rejection of the modern world. Even one of Lewis's "Vortices" in *Blast* ridiculed what he called "The Melodrama of Modernity," which he found in Italian Futurism's noisy dismissal of its classic tradition. Pound wrote that "*Blast* alone has dared to show modernity its face in an honest glass" and complained to Joyce about the difficulty of giving artistic form to "this bitched mess of modernity."[26] Eliot associated democracy with modernism, which he called a "mental blight," and warned in the Preface to *After Strange Gods*, "*Le monde moderne avilit*. It also provincialises, and it can also corrupt."[27] When he characterized "the modern mind," Eliot showed that it substituted chaotic feelings for profound belief.[28] These artists, the pioneers of modern poetry and painting, invented their new techniques to reject the modern world. Their nostalgia for an imagined past conditioned their right-wing politics. As Stephen Spender observes, "The attraction of Fascism for these writers was that it seemed a programme for using entirely modern techniques to impose upon twentieth-century society the patterns of a pre-

25. Ibid., p. 395.

26. Pound, *Pavannes and Divagations,* p. 147; Forrest Read, ed., *Pound/Joyce: Letters and Essays* (New York: New Directions, 1967), p. 148.

27. Eliot, "A Commentary," *Criterion* 8 (December 1928):188; *After Strange Gods* (New York: Harcourt, Brace, 1934), p. 9.

28. Eliot, "The Modern Mind," in *The Use of Poetry and the Use of Criticism* (London: Faber & Faber, 1933).

industrial society." [29] Even when Lewis's view of democracy mellowed after World War II, he saw modernism in art—especially surrealistic and abstract art—as a continuing threat. He attacked the antihumanism of André Malraux and complained that "the modernists pushed themselves so far out of reach of the human norm that no one could be expected to accompany them." [30]

Although a respect for tradition and the past was common to the three writers, they accused each other of merely romantic nostalgia for the past—as when Eliot attacked Pound's medievalism in *After Strange Gods.* Lewis in particular criticized Pound's and Eliot's verse for being "romantic" rather than "classic." For Lewis, Eliot's traditionalism did not show that he had the tradition from Homer onward "in his bones." Rather *The Waste Land* revealed Eliot as a "psychological romantic" who brooded on the ruins of Western culture: "And so this theory of 'the presence of the past' results in a new exoticism . . . of exactly the same order as Baudelaire's exoticism (*'les cocotiers absents de la superbe Afrique,'* etc.")." [31] To Lewis the true classical writer dealt with the here and now, with visual, tangible reality. Pound might have been defining Lewis's sense of the classical when he wrote that Joyce "is classic in that he deals with normal things and with normal people," [32] and Lewis appreciated this quality when he admired Joyce's creation of Leopold Bloom in *Ulysses.*

29. Stephen Spender, *The Struggle of the Modern* (London: Hamish Hamilton, 1936), p. 219.

30. Lewis, *The Demon of Progress in the Arts* (London: Methuen, 1954), p. 91.

31. Lewis, "Notes for *The Aristocrat,*" Olin Library, Cornell University; *Men without Art* (1934; reprinted New York: Russell & Russell, 1964), p. 73.

32. Pound, *Literary Essays,* p. 401.

Lewis thinks Eliot's advocacy of impersonality as misleading as his praise of the classical: "The 'classical' *panache* and all the rest of it, that is in the nature of a disguise . . . a bit of *le dandy* as inherited from Baudelaire and the French romantics."[33] This pretense to impersonality has a paradoxically personal effect. Lewis's argument is stated by one of the characters in *The Apes of God*: "*A mask of impersonality merely removes the obligation to be a little truly detached.* The writer like Jane Austen (her personality according to the methods of the time in full view) had that imposed upon her. . . . *The 'impersonality' of science and 'objective' observation is a wonderful patent behind which the individual can indulge in a riot of personal egotism.*"[34] Lewis concludes that there is "much more personality" in Eliot's poetry than in Pound's.[35]

Yet Pound is as harshly judged by Lewis as is Eliot, and again by the romantic-classic standard that Lewis used like shears to cut his great contemporaries down to size. Like Eliot, Pound in his verse dives for "snobbish baubles" that have "suffered a sea change into something sumptuous and odd."[36] Lewis admired Pound's poetry more than Eliot's because he considered it less sentimental and personal as well as more energetic. He credited Pound with taking Eliot "out of his lunar alley-ways and *fin-de-siècle* nocturnes."[37] One might also expect Lewis to respect Pound's aesthetics, especially his Vorticist principle that one art should not be

33. Lewis, *Men without Art,* p. 77.
34. Lewis, *The Apes of God* (1930; reprinted Baltimore: Penguin Books, 1965), p. 273.
35. Lewis, *Men without Art,* p. 68.
36. Lewis, "'One Way Song,'" quoted in Geoffrey Wagner, *Wyndham Lewis: A Portrait of the Artist as the Enemy* (New Haven: Yale University Press, 1957), p. 190.
37. Lewis, "Early London Environment," p. 31.

confounded with another. This principle led to Pound's dislike of the symbolist emphasis, so crucial to Eliot, on the musicality of poetry. In Pound's book on the composer George Antheil, he explained:

> There are two aesthetic ideals: the Wagnerian . . . i.e., you confuse the spectator by smacking as many of his senses as possible . . . this prevents his noting anything with unusual lucidity, but you may fluster or excite him to the point of making him receptive; i.e., you may slip over an emotion. . . .
>
> The other aesthetic has been approved by Brancusi, Lewis, the vorticist manifestos; it aims at focusing the mind on a given definition of form, or rhythm so intensively that it becomes not only more aware of that given form, but more sensitive to all other forms, rhythms, defined planes, or masses.[38]

In music as in poetry, Pound at least theoretically rejected vague or mysterious effects. *The Waste Land* manuscript, for example, shows that he questioned Eliot's evocative phrase "forgetful snow," which is not a visual or tangible image. In his Antheil book, Pound wrote that he disliked harmony, or "vertical" rhythm, in which lush, evocative sounds are statically arranged; he approved instead a "monolinear rhythm," in which the notation is clear and the melodic lines are dynamic. Such preferences led him to disapprove of the regularly iambic rhythm of the opening of *The Waste Land,* Part 2, and of its especially sonorous line, "Filled all the desert with inviolable voice." Pound dismissed Wagner's "pea soup" and Debussy's "heavy mist" to praise the "horizontal music" of Antheil and Igor Stravinsky, who took "hard bits of rhythm . . . noting them with great care."[39] How well do these preferences and prejudices fit Pound's practice as a poet?

38. Pound, *Antheil and the Treatise on Harmony* (New York: Da Capo Press, 1968), p. 44.
39. Ibid., p. 46.

According to Lewis, they do not fit at all. Pound's excursion into musical theory led Lewis to repudiate (temporarily but publicly) his association with his *Blast* colleague in *Time and Western Man*. The cause of Lewis's annoyance was a newspaper report that Pound and Antheil planned to "orchestrate" the sound of a factory so as to inspire the workers. Behind Pound's reported scheme Lewis detected a distrust of mere words. Lewis charged that Pound, like Paul Valéry, wanted pure musical effects in his poetry and was impatient with words because they are not musical notes: ". . . if only the words would not insist on *meaning* something. It is that that drives such poets as Pound into pure music."[40] Frank Kermode was to repeat this charge a generation later in his *Romantic Image.* Lewis believed that Pound's technique in *The Cantos,* which Pound himself likened to the art of the fugue, was akin to Gertrude Stein's "attempt to use words as though . . . their symbolism could be distorted or suppressed sufficiently to allow of a 'fugue' being made out of a few thousand of them." Since words necessarily mean something, Lewis concluded that Pound committed the unforgivable sin (for a Vorticist) of being "lost halfway between one art and another."[41]

A symptom of this distrust of words is the incantatory quality of Pound's verse, as in this passage from Canto 17, which Lewis cites in *Time and Western Man*:

Cave of Nerea,
    she like a great shell curved,
And the boat drawn without sound,
Without odour of ship-work,
Nor bird-cry, nor any noise of wave moving,
Nor splash of porpoise, nor any noise of wave moving,

40. Lewis, *Time and Western Man* (London: Chatto & Windus, 1927), p. 197.
41. Ibid., p. 131.

> Within her cave, Nerea,
>> she like a great shell curved . . .

Lewis called the technique of this passage the "repetitive hypnotic method." Although Pound condemned the aesthetic that prevents the reader from "noting anything with unusual clarity," Lewis believed that Pound's own "hypnotic method" lulls the reader and so prevents lucidity. And indeed Pound's sea nymph does hover on the fringe of consciousness in the way Stéphane Mallarmé's nymphs do in *L'Après-midi d'un faune.* Nevertheless, the weakness of Lewis's criticism is that he was unable to appreciate the specific kind of lucidity Pound desired.

In his Vorticist poetry, Pound did note "hard bits of rhythm" and create "hard-edged" images, as in "The Game of Chess," which first appeared in the 1915 issue of *Blast*:

> Red Knights, brown bishops, bright queens,
> Striking the board, falling in strong "L's" of
>> colour
> Reaching and striking in angles,
>> holding lines in one colour.[42]

Although there is great precision here, the images are conventional and the rhythm inflexible; the participles give a mere illusion of activity and excitement. In Canto 2, however, the same precision and lucidity characterize images of far greater power:

> Glare azure of water, cold-welter, close cover.
> Quiet sun-tawny sand-stretch,
> The gulls broad out their wings,
>> nipping between the splay feathers;
> Snipe come for their bath
>> bend out their wing-joints . . .

42. Pound, *Personae* (New York: New Directions, 1971), p. 120.

Surely this is lucid enough, one might conclude, even for Wyndham Lewis. Unlike the Nerea of Canto 17, the birds are precisely rendered by such notations as "splay feathers" and "wing-joints." The staccato phrases of the first line vividly set the scene, and Vorticist "word-apposition" is brilliantly used in such combinations as "sun-tawny," "cold-welter," and the razor-edged "glare azure." Yet the very power of these images, when compared to the chessboard image, would be suspect to Lewis. Not only does the passage drum out the kind of hypnotic rhythm that Lewis disparaged in the Cave of Nerea passage; it also leads to the perception of another world, one of Pound's "moments of metamorphosis," which blots out the spatial, material world to which Lewis dedicated his art. And so in Canto 2, in one of these timeless, spaceless moments,

> There is a wine-red glow in the shallows,
> a tin flash in the sun-dazzle.

Such moments are as intrinsic to Pound's romantic art as the "spots of time" are to Wordsworth's.

The lucidity of Canto 2 is that of a dream, which indeed helps to account for the power of its images when compared to those in "The Game of Chess." It is the lucidity of Valéry's "Le Cimetière marin" or of this passage from Mallarmé's "Prose pour des Esseintes":

> Oui, dans une île que l'air charge
> De vue et non de visions
> Toute fleur s'étalait plus large. . . .[43]

This is Pound's (and Valéry's in "Le Cimetière") clear Mediterranean world. The magical experience derives from pre-

43. Stéphane Mallarmé, "Prose pour des Esseintes," *The Penguin Book of French Verse,* III (Baltimore: Penguin Books, 1957), p. 199.

cise notation of visual details. They are no mere visions but realities perceived with a "primitive" directness and freshness. Lewis accurately showed that Pound was developing in the practice of his poetry a romantic and symbolist tradition that he rejected in his criticism. This development, however, was not the defect Lewis imagined it to be. Pound's absorption of the symbolist tradition demonstrates his ability to profit from a movement he considered a rival of Imagism and Vorticism.

When one turns from Lewis's criticism to his art, whether visual or verbal, the split between what he says and what he does is more gaping in his work than in Ezra Pound's. The opening pages of Lewis's *Childermass* (which Yeats in praising described as "the first region of the dead as the ghosts everywhere describe it")[44] and the descriptive passages in *The Apes of God* are powerful precisely because of their oneiric lucidity. Thus in *The Childermass,* "The delicate surf falls with the abrupt crash of glass, section by section."[45] Lewis's late novel *Self Condemned* is "expressionist fiction," as Hugh Kenner calls it, "as wholly absorbing as a dream while we are dreaming it."[46] In his paintings, Lewis's nonportrait art developed a complicated dream aesthetic and sometimes even reproduced images from his own dreams, as in his *Departure of a Princess from Chaos.*[47] Such canvases as *Mud Clinic, The Armada,* and *The Surrender of Barcelona,* as well as the *Creation Myths* that span his entire career as

44. Yeats, *The Letters of W. B. Yeats,* ed. Allen Wade (London: Rupert Hart-Davis, 1954), p. 745.
45. Lewis, *The Childermass* (London: Chatto & Windus, 1928), p. 34.
46. Hugh Kenner, "Introduction," in Lewis, *Self Condemned* (Chicago: Henry Regnery, 1965), p. xii, vii.
47. Lewis, "Foreword: Paintings and Drawings by Wyndham Lewis," in Walter Michel, *Wyndham Lewis: Paintings and Drawings* (Berkeley and Los Angeles: University of California Press, 1971), p. 440.

an artist, are organized with the freedom from conventional and logical limits one enjoys or suffers in a dream. If the appropriate formal design for a painting, such as *Stations of the Dead,* requires one of its figures to float away from the horizontal plane or its head to be geometrically rounded, the alteration takes place as inevitably as the events of a dream are altered to fit the dream's design. Similarly, the ships that emerge from the upper left background of *Stations* and from the upper right of *Departure of a Princess* are visually right, however puzzling their presence is. Lewis saw a similarity in art and dreams: "Dreams are an example of sensations evolved, with great complexity, in a new order, and with new emotional stresses and juxtapositions. The work of the dramatist or novelist is in this category, and that of most painters whose work is remembered. But the work of art does the re-ordering in the interests of the intellect as well as of the emotions."[48] Lewis's reference to the "interest of the intellect" indicates the emphasis that keeps Lewis from the brink of surrealism. But this emphasis on intellectual or conscious control does not limit his Romanticism. Like Blake in Yeats's phrase, Lewis is "a too literal realist of imagination." Lewis's dream pictures stress the order and clarity of the visual experience over its mysteriousness. Although his precise delineation of form resembles Giorgio di Chirico's, he does not cultivate moods of melancholy, ennui, or terror in the manner of the Italian painter. Lewis shares with Chirico an admiration, by no means common in modern painters, for the High Renaissance and a bold ambition to paint on the scale and with the confidence of an Old Master. Many of Lewis's paintings, such as *AΘA-NATON* (1933), appear to be allegorical paintings to which

48. *Wyndham Lewis on Art,* p. 215.

the allegorical references are lost, works in some great tradition that does not exist.[49] In such works, Lewis's dreamlike reordering "in the interest of the intellect" severely limits the effect of works whose iconography is necessarily obscure and in which the inherent emotional power of the forms are far less than Chirico's mannikins and city squares. One feels the difference between the two painters when comparing Lewis's *Surrender of Barcelona* (1936) with Chirico's much earlier *Philosopher's Conquest* (1914). The massive architectural forms and sailing ships of Lewis's painting do not open into the mysterious perspective that similar forms introduce in Chirico's work. Nor do any of the forms in Lewis's work have the authority and stubby presence of Chirico's artichokes in the same painting. The paintings in which Lewis presents some primitive rite, such as *Departure of a Princess, Stations of the Dead,* and *Red Figures Carrying Babies and Visiting Graves,* have greater emotional impact than his wholly abstract or architectural canvases. Yet Lewis does not draw the viewer into the rite he presents. His interest in the scene is that of of an anthropologist who can transcribe but not penetrate the rite unfolding before him. Although he was not a true anti-Romantic any more than Pound was, Lewis could have profited from a still greater measure of Romantic emotionalism.

Augustus John said that Lewis was a "Romantic *in flight from himself.*"[50] The same may be said of the authors of *The Cantos* and of that quest for the timeless moment, *Four Quartets.* T. S. Eliot came to a sensible conclusion about the Romantic/classic debate when he said it was "easier to be a classicist in literary criticism than in creative art—because in

49. See Hugh Kenner's interpretation of this painting in ibid., p. 26.
50. Augustus John, *Finishing Touches,* ed. Daniel George (London: George Cape, 1964), p. 121.

criticism you are responsible only for what you want, and in creation you are responsible for what you can do with material which you must simply accept."[51] In a similarly candid mood, Lewis admitted: "To be impersonal rather than personal; universal rather than provincial; rational rather than a mere creature of feeling—those . . . are very fine things indeed: but who possesses more than a tincture of them today? . . . With all of us—and to this there is no exception—there are merely *degrees* of the opposite tendency, at present labeled 'romantic.'"[52]

Although Pound, Eliot, and Lewis were guardians of tradition, a tradition more flexibly interpreted with the years, they were not the mandarins or high priests of art they have sometimes been called. They considered themselves professionals who were developing a tradition of complete dedication to craft. Donald Davie has contrasted Pound's and Lewis's professionalism to the countertradition of the amateur in Edwardian England: "Both Pound and Lewis were American or Americanized enough to have on the contrary a *professional* attitude to their respective arts, in the quite precise sense that they saw the continuity of the art-traditions ensured by the *atelier,* the master instructing his prentices."[53] Davie's reference to Lewis as "Americanized" is indeed crucial to Lewis's professionalism, and Pound himself was delighted to learn, some years after their first meeting, that Lewis had been born in North America (Nova Scotia). Lewis recalled that when he told Pound of his origins, "he laughed a great deal—'Oh if the *deah* British public only knew that *three* Americans—he, Eliot, and self—were responsible for all this

51. Eliot, "'Ulysses', Order, and Myth," in *Selected Prose of T. S. Eliot,* ed. Frank Kermode (New York: Harcourt Brace Jovanovich, 1975), p. 177.
52. Lewis, *Men without Art,* pp. 193–94.
53. Donald Davie, "Ezra among the Edwardians," *Paideuma* 5 (Spring–Summer 1976):9.

disturbance, *Blasting, Imagism, Vorticism*! etc.' said he—very amused."[54]

Lewis himself founded *The Tyro,* as he explained in its first issue, in order to provide "a rallying spot for those painters" for whom art was "a constant and perpetually renewed effort: requiring as exacting and intelligent application as any science, with as great an aim."[55] *The Tyro's* second issue carried Eliot's attack on the British amateur tradition: "One may even say that the present situation here has now become a national scandal impossible to conceal from foreign nations; that literature is chiefly in the hands of persons who may be interested in almost anything else. . . . The British writer, who shrinks from working overtime or at weekends, will not find these ideas congenial."[56] Pound seems to echo Eliot's final phrase when he claims that "it is impossible to talk about perfection without getting yourself very much disliked."[57] Pound's bitter remark is in turn the theme of the comment Eliot made in 1949 to John Rothenstein when they were leaving an exhibition of Lewis's paintings: "Eliot . . . spoke with admiration of Lewis, but observed that one of the reasons certain people so disliked him was that he was a 'pro,' both as writer and painter."[58]

This sense that professional excellence itself provokes hostility, which in Lewis became the vision of tyros or apes gathering to mock the godlike artist, indicates how embattled the Vortex pros felt throughout their careers. In a reminiscence of the *Blast* days, Pound used a Vortex image to

54. Lewis, *Letters,* p. 464.
55. Lewis, "The Objects of This Paper," *Tyro,* no. 1 (1921), p. 2.
56. Eliot, "The Three Provincialities," *Tyro,* no. 2 (1922), pp. 12–13.
57. Pound, *Literary Essays,* p. 371.
58. John Rothenstein, *Autobiography,* vol. 3, *Time's Thievish Progress* (London: Cassell, 1970), pp. 39–40.

complain that the real artist "is bound to suffer occulta-
tion . . . because men of little comprehension cannot reconcile
themselves to . . . intelligence shining in divers places from a
center."[59] Anyone who tries to assemble a knot of intelligent
people will be punished for it, he wrote in 1920, thinking no
doubt of the way he was blockaded from the *Quarterly
Review* because his association with *Blast* stamped "a man
too disadvantageously."[60] According to Hugh Kenner, the
boycott by the *Quarterly* did "long-term psychic damage" to
Pound's mind, though in acknowledging this distress one
should not underestimate the impact of Gaudier's death,
which Pound said "obsessed" him for a time.[61] Although
Pound was adjudged by a panel of government-appointed
psychiatrists as "suffering from a paranoid state,"[62] a life
spent trying to earn a living writing poetry and prose for
intellectual magazines gave Pound sufficient reason to feel
persecuted. The best rate he generally received after being
closed off from the *Quarterly* was a mere guinea a page from
Eliot's *Criterion*. Eliot described Pound's economic hardship
when he wrote to John Quinn about the need for a publishing outlet for Pound and Lewis, "the only writers in London
whose work is worth publishing": "The fact is that there is
now no organ of any importance in which [Pound] . . . can
express himself, and he is becoming forgotten. It is not
enough for him simply to publish a volume of verse once a

59. Pound, "D'Artagnan Twenty Years After," *Criterion* 16 (July
1937):608.
60. Pound, *Literary Essays,* p. 357.
61. Hugh Kenner, *The Pound Era* (Berkeley and Los Angeles: University of California Press, 1971), p. 244; Pound, *Selected Letters of Ezra
Pound, 1907–1941,* ed. D. D. Paige (New York: New Directions, 1950), p.
61.
62. C. David Heymann, *Ezra Pound: The Last Rower* (New York:
Viking Press, 1976), p. 190.

year . . . for it will simply not be reviewed, and will be killed by silence."[63]

Pound referred to himself as a "banned writer" and Lewis called himself a "half-suppressed" one.[64] The "conspiracy of silence" that Lewis claimed was against him was admittedly deafening at times, as in the case of the furor Lewis raised when *The New Statesman* rejected Roy Campbell's favorable review of *The Apes of God*.[65] Lewis's very overreactions to criticisms and snubs in time provoked very real hostility and neglect. His temperament was defensive to the point of paranoia. His obsessive concern with the outsides of a thing, with his "external approach" to fictional characters and portrait subjects, schematized his experiences to give him the precarious illusion that he controlled them. Naturally, people did not care to be so rigidly categorized; nor did events stand still long enough to validate Lewis's brilliant but frequently wrong analyses. Yet we can call Eliot to witness that Lewis, whatever his own fault in this matter, was "persistently ignored or deprecated" because the art and literary establishment "did not find him congenial."[66] Walter Allen's sensitive comment on Lewis's "paranoid tendencies" is applicable to Pound's case as well: "The persecution-mania was no doubt self-destructive; but as one reads [Lewis's letters], as indeed when one met him, what sticks out is not the persecution-mania but the energy and the heroism that were its concomitants and that enabled him to triumph over neglect, illness,

63. Quoted in Donald Gallup, *T. S. Eliot and Ezra Pound: Collaborators in Letters* (New Haven: Henry W. Wenning, 1970), p. 15.
64. Pound, "Mr Eliot's Solid Merit," *New English Weekly* 13 (July 12, 1934):298; Lewis, *Rude Assignment* (London: Hutchinson, 1950), p. 194.
65. See Lewis's *Satire and Fiction* (London: Arthur Press, 1930).
66. Quoted in Walter Allen, "Lonely Old Volcano," *Encounter* 21 (September 1963):63.

poverty. . . ."[67] This "paranoia" was related not only to the energy of Lewis's and Pound's psyches but also to their great, eccentric powers of synthesis in *Time and Western Man* and *The Cantos* (or, to glance at another artist with a persecution complex, to Joyce's powers in *Finnegans Wake*).

Whether one sees Pound, Eliot, and Lewis as professionals or as near paranoids, one notices the strained relation to their audiences throughout their careers. The concept of the Vortex implied that a culture's most vital ideas would be gathered in the Vortex and brought to a still point of clarity. Yet the *Blast* group was not at first concerned with reaching a wide audience. Its initial goal was to form a rallying point for the avant-garde, and it was content to shock rather than inform the public. The public's shocked reception of *Blast*, however, was more than the Rebels bargained for. Referring to the furor over *Blast*, Pound asked, "Does anything but the need of food drive the artist into contact with the homo canis?"[68] When Lewis and Pound wrote a series of "Imaginary Letters" for *The Little Review*, whose masthead carried the slogan "Making No Compromise with the Public Taste," the shared theme was that the artist must keep himself above the "herd." This aggressiveness, or defensiveness, infected Pound's style, as he himself noticed in criticizing his "big stick habit": "Joyce is a writer, I tell you . . . Lewis can paint . . . WIPE your feet!!!!!!"[69]

Pound and Lewis often rushed out their prose for quick consumption in order to air their opinions or slap down apes. When Lewis complained about the quality of Pound's

67. Ibid., p. 53.
68. Pound, *Pavannes and Divagations*, p. 148.
69. Pound, *Selected Letters*, pp. 122–23.

Instigations, Pound replied that it was not meant for Lewis to read but for "barbarous Americans": "Our opinion of Instig. can only be that it is crowd-police work, intended to keep the mob in order; and that opinion shd. be kept to ourselves."[70] Lewis's disastrous political books, such as *Count Your Dead: They Are Alive!* and *Hitler,* resulted from such "crowd-police work," as well as from the necessity, which Pound shared, of producing quick commentaries on topical issues for the money they would bring. Lewis's habit of bolting long quotations, ranging from newspaper articles to the prose of Alfred North Whitehead, into unrevised chapters or essays at times makes his work seem a parody of the "ideogrammic method." His taste for schematizing and exaggerating the stands of his opponents and for overstating his own case, which he once called his "antinomic" style, is already found in the "Blasts" and "Blesses" of contemporary figures that were one of the scandalous features of *Blast.*[71]

Eliot's style of course was more cultivated than Pound's or Lewis's. Pound thought this was partly the result of his advice: "I pointed out to him in the beginning there was no use of two of us butting a stone wall; that he wd. never be as hefty a battering ram as I was, nor as explosive as Lewis, and that he'd better try a more oceanic and fluid method of sapping the foundations."[72] In a more positive mood, Pound once said that he threw rocks in the window while Eliot stole in and made off with the swag.[73] Pound thought Eliot's "keerful Criterese" was a facade meant to hide the live ideas

70. Pound to Lewis, n.d. (early 1920s), Olin Library, Cornell University.
71. For identification of the objects of the "Blasts" and "Blesses," see William C. Wees, *Vorticism and the English Avant-Garde* (Manchester: Manchester University Press, 1972).
72. Quoted in Gallup, *T. S. Eliot and Ezra Pound,* p. 28.
73. Cited in William H. Pritchard, *Wyndham Lewis* (New York: Twayne Publishers, 1968), p. 56.

that he was insinuating into insular minds and to protect him "in the stinking and foggy climik agin the bare-boreians."[74] In the long run, however, Pound thought that Eliot "outmaneuvered" himself. He blamed the caution of Eliot's prose, which might rather be interpreted as a respect for one's audience, on an elitist spirit: "His contempt for his readers has always been much greater than mine, by which I would indicate that I quite often write as if I expected my reader to use his intelligence . . . [whereas] Mr. Eliot after enduring decennial fogs in Britain practically always writes as if for very feeble and brittle mentalities."[75] Eliot implicitly answered this charge in his complaint to Pound about an article on economics which he had commissioned for *The Criterion*. Eliot told Pound that he wanted something "which would explain this subject to people who had never heard of it; yet you write as if your readers knew about it already, but had failed to understand it."[76] In a letter of 1934 he told Pound that he couldn't expect *The Criterion*'s readers to be excited about the financial policies of Martin Van Buren and Nicholas Biddle any more than Americans would be over the foreign policy of Viscount Castlereagh.[77] As Pound's editor at Faber, Eliot was constantly irritated by Pound's obscurity and potential libels. Whatever condescension or snobbery one detects in Eliot's prose, Eliot knew better than Pound how to reach an audience. Yet Pound should have the last word on this matter, for he sensibly inquired, "Has Eliot or have I wasted the greater number of hours, he by attending to fools and/or humouring them, and I by alienating imbe-

74. Pound, *Selected Letters,* p. 302.
75. Pound, "Appendix II," in *Confucius to Cummings,* ed. Ezra Pound and Marcella Spann (New York: New Directions, 1964), p. 333; Pound, *Active Anthology,* p. 9.
76. Eliot, "Ezra Pound," *Poetry* 68 (September 1946):336.
77. Eliot to Pound, January 12, 1934, Beinecke Library, Yale University.

ciles suddenly?"[78] The truth is that Pound, Eliot, and Lewis all wasted time and talent because of their troubled relationships with their audiences.

In mid-careers all three artists not only began to lament their lack of a popular audience but also considered methods of winning one. In 1932 Eliot worried about the value of setting down feelings that, "if communicable at all, can be communicated to so few that the result seems insignificant compared to the labor."[79] This statement seems surprising from the author of *The Waste Land,* which by defying a popular audience found, even when first published, something like Milton's "fit audience . . . though few." Eliot was more justified in complaining that "the more serious authors have a limited, and even provincial audience."[80] According to Lewis, this limited audience results from the corruption of the "Majority Public" by "monopoly-capital and mass-production"—a judgment that Pound shared. And Lewis was as unhappy with the minority public as Eliot:

> Our present-day Minority Public is not a half, probably only a tenth, of the Eighteenth Century Public. It is the Public of the Intelligentsia. Although much smaller, this Public of the Intelligentsia might be expected to compare favourably with the Public of the aristocratic era. That is, however, not the case. It is too specialised: an unrepresentative fraction of the whole. And it *is* the whole, in some form or other, that is required by a writer.[81]

Lewis saw no way to capture this "whole" or more representative audience, though he was gratified by the success that

78. Pound, *Guide to Kulchur* (New York: New Directions, 1968), p. 177.
79. Eliot, "Christianity and Communism," *Listener* 7 (March 16, 1932):382.
80. Eliot, *Selected Prose* (New York: Harcourt Brace Jovanovich, 1975), p. 289.
81. Lewis, *Rude Assignment,* pp. 21, 16.

several of his novels enjoyed when dramatized by the BBC. Eliot reached a wider audience with his plays, notably *The Cocktail Party.* In praising Shakespeare's appeal to a large and varied audience, Eliot expressed his conviction that the drama is "the most direct means of social 'usefulness' for poetry."[82] When Pound heard *Murder in the Cathedral* on the radio in 1936, he remarked that "Mizzr Shakzpeer *still* retains his posishun."[83] In mellower years Pound praised the language of Eliot's later plays for "being able to make contact with an extant milieu, and an extant state of comprehension."[84] Pound was unable to reach this "extant milieu" with his *Cantos.* As Hugh Kenner has observed, *The Cantos* never gained even a specialized audience between the wars; no body of contemporary criticism developed around the poems as it did around *The Waste Land* and *Ulysses.*[85] Eliot noted an "increasing defect of communication"[86] in Pound that defeated even the kind of specialized audience that greeted *The Waste Land.* One of Pound's most obscure volumes, *Rock-Drill* cantos, nevertheless represents for Pound an attempt to reach a public, as one sees in the following comment to Lewis: "ROCK DRILL, whence the title on my last attempt to drill something into the pliocine occiput of the b. bloody pup Lick."[87] Years later he said of *The Cantos,* "There is no doubt that the writing is too obscure as it stands, but I hope the order of ascension in the Paradiso is toward a greater limpidity."[88] He attained this "limpidity"

82. Eliot, *Selected Prose,* p. 94.
83. Pound, *Selected Letters,* p. 277.
84. "Ezra Pound: An Interview," *Paris Review* 28 (Summer–Fall 1962):37.
85. Kenner, *Pound Era,* p. 415.
86. Eliot, "Ezra Pound," *Poetry,* September 1946, p. 336.
87. Pound to Lewis, August 2, 1956, Olin Library, Cornell University.
88. "Ezra Pound: An Interview," p. 49.

for the final, paradisical stage of *The Cantos* only in fragments, however, in such delicate images as one finds in his
elegy for Lewis: "a pale flare over marshes / where the salt
hay whispers to tide's change" (Canto 115).

Their common concern with craft, tradition, and social
responsibility united Pound, Eliot, and Lewis for more than
forty years. But their increasing anxiety over their audience
was just one sign that the Vortex lost some of its aggressive
force and confidence with the years. After World War II,
their association—no longer anything so energetic as a
vortex—continued in years of relative peace. Lewis wrote of
Pound's career in *Self Condemned* and "Doppelgänger: A
Story"; he provided the title for Pound's *Rock-Drill* cantos,
and Pound in turn suggested the name Rotting Hill (in
reference to Lewis's London district, Notting Hill) which
became the title for Lewis's 1951 collection of stories. While
Pound was imprisoned in St. Elizabeths Hospital, Eliot and
Lewis did what they could to free him, though they worried
over what new trouble the unrepentant poet might get into if
he were released. Eliot helped Lewis through the time when
Lewis discovered, with certainty in 1951, that he was going
blind. Eliot loaned him the money to consult Swiss eye
specialists and, when his eyesight completely failed, read
proofs for Lewis's late work *The Human Age.*

Lewis was the first of the three to die—in 1957, of the
tumor that had taken his sight. Pound immediately began to
organize a memorial issue of *Edge* for him, which never
materialized. Canto 115, however, with its opening reference
to Lewis's intellectual integrity and energy ("Wyndham
Lewis chose blindness / rather than have his mind stop") is a
more than sufficient memorial. One of Pound's comments on
Eliot's death in 1968 is recorded by Robert Lowell:

"And who is left to understand my jokes?
My old brother in the arts . . ."[89]

It was as if Pound's true audience were a few close friends who were now lost. In *Drafts & Fragments* (Canto 110) he wrote, with a beautiful echo of *The Waste Land:*

> all the resisters blacked out,
> From time's wreckage shored
> these fragments shored against ruin . . .

Eliot thought that "*if* poetry is a form of 'communication', yet that which is to be communicated is the poem itself."[90] In the same sense, the meaning of the Vortex is the entire history of these three artists' careers. Eliot meant something like this when he wrote, in the lines that are engraved on his Westminster cenotaph:

> the communication
> Of the dead is tongued with fire beyond the language
> of the living.[91]

The meaning is found on the disordered rim of the Vortex, in their brave but often embittered campaigns in the fields of philosophy and politics, but also in the still center of their achievements as artists. The energy to explore the modern world and the will to press their discoveries upon the public characterizes their work. They escaped the "dissociation" and defied the "dispossession" of the modern artist.

89. Robert Lowell, "Ezra Pound," in *Notebook: Revised and Expanded Edition* (New York: Farrar, Straus & Giroux, 1970), p. 119.
90. Eliot, *Selected Prose,* p. 80.
91. Eliot, "Little Gidding," I, in *Collected Poems, 1909–1962* (New York: Harcourt Brace Jovanovich, 1963), p. 201.

Index

Numbers in italics indicate pages where illustrations appear.

Index

Index

VORTEX

Designed by Richard E. Rosenbaum.
Composed by Jessamy Graphics, Inc.
in 11 point Times Roman, 3 points leaded,
with display lines in Times Roman and Tiffany Heavy.
Printed offset by Thomson/Shore, Inc. on
Warren's Olde Style, 60 pound basis.
Bound by John H. Dekker & Sons, Inc.
in Holliston book cloth and
stamped in All Purpose foil.

Library of Congress Cataloging in Publication Data

Materer, Timothy, 1940–
  Vortex.

  Includes index.
  1. American poetry—20th century—History and criticism. 2. Vorticism—Great
Britain. 3. Pound, Ezra Loomis, 1885–1972—Criticism and interpretation. 4. Eliot,
Thomas Stearns, 1888–1965—Criticism and interpretation. 5. Lewis, Wyndham,
1882–1957—Criticism and interpretation. I. Title.
PS324.M37   820'.9'00912   79-13009
ISBN 0-8014-1225-0